Migration, Identity and Conflict

Migration, Identity and Conflict

Lived Experience of Northeasterners in Delhi

Tiplut Nongbri
A.S. Shimreiwung

RAWAT PUBLICATIONS
Jaipur • New Delhi • Bangalore • Guwahati • Kolkata

ISBN 978-81-316-0852-4

Published by
Prem Rawat for **Rawat Publications**
Satyam Apts, Sector 3, Jawahar Nagar, Jaipur 302 004 (India)
Phone: 0141 265 1748 / 7006 Fax: 0141 265 1748
E-mail: info@rawatbooks.com
Website: www.rawatbooks.com

New Delhi Office
4858/24, Ansari Road, Daryaganj, New Delhi 110 002
Phone: 011 2326 3290

Also at *Bangalore, Guwahati* and *Kolkata*

Typeset by Rawat Computers, Jaipur
Printed at Chaman Enterprises, New Delhi

Contents

Preface

The materials that provide the basis of this book came from a study carried out under the North-East India Studies Programme, Jawaharlal Nehru University, New Delhi as a response to the barrage of media reports and public anxiety at the violence perpetrated on the people of Northeast India living, and working in the metropolitan cities of the country. The movement of people from the Northeastern states to cities across India, in the hope of improving their educational and professional prospects, has steadily increased in recent times. This form of migration, in terms of its scale and proportion, has been unprecedented so far as the people from Northeast are concerned.

Moving beyond what is popularly perceived as 'racial discrimination', the book focuses on the lived experience of Northeast migrants at the level of the quotidian, looking in particular at the intricacies of intercommunity relations, the social bonding and disjuncture, and modes of adaptation and adjustment that are bound to occur when people of different cultures are forced to share common space. While we have liberally drawn from various theories to make sense of our materials, we have refrained from situating the analysis within tight theoretical formulation, as this runs the risk of diluting the facts and integrity of the narrative. The data for the book has been sourced primarily from Delhi, which is one of the most favoured destinations for persons from Northeast migrating to the cities. Given the nature and scope of the subject, we hope this should not be a limiting factor and readers find it useful to understand the problem on a larger scale.

We are grateful to JNU for providing the initial financial assistance for this work. We also express our thankfulness to the field investigators who helped us in the initial phase of data collection by administering the questionnaire to the respondents. We would also like to place on record our gratitude to the respondents who answered the questionnaires and to the very many others who despite their tight schedule readily gave their time to share their experience with us during the extended fieldwork.

A special 'thank you' to Dr Manjeet Baruah, for his constant support and constructive comments on the initial draft, and to Romeo Hmar, Maivo Wobha and L. Lamkhanpiang for sharing the letters and some of the photographs used in the text.

Our thanks also go to Mr Pranit Rawat and his team at Rawat Publications for the care with which they handled the publication of this book.

None of the persons named and unnamed are responsible for the content or views expressed in the book, the responsibility for which lie solely with the authors.

New Delhi
9 February 2017

Tiplut Nongbri
A.S. Shimreiwung

Chapter 1

Introduction

The Northeastern region which is generally considered as 'isolated' and 'remote' from the rest of the country due to its geographical location, poor connectivity and different cultural practices has always evoked a sense of *strangeness* in the dominant communities of India. However, the opening up of the region to the rest of the country and other parts of the world is taking place in an incredible manner, with people from the region migrating in large numbers to distant places in search of higher education and employment opportunities. The phenomenon of human migration and its related problems has been a burning issue for most of the Northeastern states; however, 'in-migration' to the Northeast has been the focal point of attention in the past. In recent times, the widely reported problems of discrimination faced by people from Northeast in cities across India have brought the phenomenon of 'out-migration' to the fore, which has made it a major cause of concern for the central and state governments in the region.

Although the pull and push factors have generally been the focal point of attention in migration studies, there is an urgent need to go beyond these factors as recent studies have indicated that the migrant's presentation of the 'self' generally revolve round their homeland, no matter how far they may have travelled out. The desire to remain rooted within one's own community has not only determined their venture in career and earnings, but also shaped the social relations they established in the cities and distant places where they have settled down.

The mode of social and cultural interaction between people from Northeast and other parts of the country during the process of 'settling down' in urban cities calls for detailed analysis. In recent times, atrocities against people from the Northeast have made headlines in both the print and electronic media. Media has projected these acts of violence against the Northeasterners as a result of 'stereotyping', 'racism', 'cultural alienation' and so on. However, the lived experiences of people from the Northeast in cities such as Delhi have not been sufficiently explored. Issues such as how do they conduct their daily life and the challenges they face have not been systematically examined. The urban social spaces, such as residential areas, offices, educational institutions, markets, public transport and communication systems – where modes of accommodation by the host community with the people from Northeast and acculturation by Northeasterners are increasingly taking place need to be closely examined in order to grasp the larger dimension of the problem. While the outbreak of certain forms of atrocities against the people from Northeast India has been widely publicized by the media, the problem is yet to be taken seriously by social scientists and policy makers. This work is a humble attempt to look further into the issue and interrogate the problems from within. For such analysis, perception of the people and their construction of themselves and the 'other' served a good starting point through which the process of intercommunity relationships are established.

Some scholars and activists have argued that 'racial profiling', where an opinion or a perspective is formed on a group of people based on their physical appearance, culture and life ways, has been the root cause of discrimination against the people from Northeast. The geographical and racial proximity of the region to Southeast Asia is routinely invoked to demarcate its people from the rest of the Indian population. Further, the official categorization of a large number of communities in the Northeast as Scheduled Tribes, and the associated perception that tribes are steeped in 'backwardness' and 'primitivism', has deepened the divide between the people of Northeast and 'mainland' India. Although the demographic composition of the Northeastern region is predominantly non-tribal,[1] Northeasterners have generally been looked at as tribes, or possessing and exhibiting tribal characteristics.

Interestingly, what constitutes 'tribal characteristics', analysis reveals, are a mix of racial stereotypes and ideological and moral prejudices. Though the Indian Constitution, which provides the legal base for the categorization of a people or community as Scheduled Tribe, nowhere spells out the definition of 'tribe', data gathered by Joy Pachuau from a village in Delhi for her doctoral research at the University of Oxford reveals that as tribes Northeasterners are not only considered as ritually 'inferior' to Hindus, but also seen as 'dirty' because they consume 'unclean' food, such as pork and beef. Besides, the relatively liberal attitude Northeasterners display towards the intermingling of the sexes and the use of Western attire have also brought them under the censorious eyes of the local community. Associating choice of clothing and style with morality, women from Northeast are often considered to be of 'loose moral character' (Pachuau, 2010: 52), a trait our findings show goes against the conservative ethos of the local population. That the behaviour of the Northeasterners (majority of whom are students) is not very dissimilar to the behaviour of many educated youth from upwardly mobile middle-class homes in the city, appears to be lost on the local community. What further reinforces the otherness of the Northeasterners in the eyes of the locals is the people's widespread adoption of Christianity, with its cult of church and prayer, and propensity to steer the youth away from assimilation with the dominant Hindu population.

The conceptualization of the people of Northeast as the social and cultural 'other' in popular imagination while it vividly brings out the gulf that characterizes the relations between the Northeasterners and the host society, it also obscures the internal variation that divides the Northeast society along the lines of language, tribe and ethnicity, which poses constraints to their coming together as a community. It is the endeavour of this book to focus its attention on both these aspects. While our primary endeavour is to closely examine how the cultural distance between the Northeast migrants and the host society is played out at the level of the quotidian, equal attention is paid to the pattern of interaction within the migrant community to arrive at a better understanding of how and to what extent migration into the city has helped the Northeasterners bridge the internal divide that exists among them.

In historical terms, the process of Christianization-cum-Westernization had already taken place in the various tribal societies of Northeast, much before they ventured out of their homeland. And shared socio-cultural spaces may have established some common cultural traits among the diverse communities, which may remain unnoticed by them but visible to the other communities. Thus, perceptions towards Northeasterners and their cultural practices by the locals in cities have been different from the way Northeasterners look at themselves and their relation to each other's community. One aspect where such diversified perceptions formed by Northeasterners living in the city can be discerned is from the manner in which they have formed numerous tribe and ethnic-based social institutions and organizations to cater to the needs of the respective communities.

The social moorings of the Northeasterners in Delhi, where the bonding and identity of communities residing outside their native states are being strengthened, have not been given the importance it deserves in either the academia or institution of governance. Set against this backdrop, attempts have been made to look into the social mediums through which people from Northeast have established their community identity and strive to maintain the relationship with other communities while living in Delhi. As an extension of this attempt, special attention has been paid to the social, cultural and religious institutions that have been established to maintain tribal cohesion and identities by different groups and in different platforms. There was also the need to look into the construction of the community identity and boundaries that influences the intercommunity relationships between the local population and Northeasterners. Difference with respect to food habits and religious values between the Northeasterners and other communities also required close analysis for understanding the intricacies in social distance.

Harassment meted out to women has been prominently highlighted when it comes to the issue of discrimination of the Northeasterners in the city. Frequent media reports on sexual harassment and violence experienced by Northeast women at the hands of landlords, employers and sundry others have projected them as 'soft-targets' for the social deviants. In a survey conducted by the Centre for North East Studies and Policy Research (CNESPR) on Northeast women in four cities – Delhi, Kolkata, Bengaluru and Mumbai – it is revealed that 60 per cent women experienced varying forms of discrimination in their everyday life. The city-wise distribution of figures shows that Delhi tops the list at 81 per cent, followed by Bengaluru at 60 per cent and Mumbai at 46 per cent. The least discrimination is recorded in Kolkata at 42 per cent (CNESPR, 2014: 43).[2] This raises the question, what accounts for the vulnerability of Northeast women? Is this a simple consequence of their gender or does it constitute a part of the general conception and 'stereotyping' of people from Northeast?

While gender discriminations and sexual assaults on women continue to be one of the major problems that Northeasterners face in Delhi, other forms of harassments and discriminations towards the people from Northeast have also seen an upward rise. But these have yet to be given due cognizance by analysts. The one-sided representation in the media has also obscured the social relations that people from Northeast have with their host society and fellow migrants in cities like Delhi. The focus has generally been more on issues that have high sensational value and scant attention paid to their social and cultural life and the day-to-day experience of the people at the micro level.

This book has tried to go beyond what has been generally understood as the problems of Northeasterners in the cities with special focus on the lived experiences of people in their everyday life, the dynamics of living in a locality, sharing the social and working spaces with different sections of people from other communities. Specifically, it looks into the pattern of relationship between the people from Northeast and the dominant population to find out the 'social distance' and 'closeness' between them.

Objectives

The study, which provides the theoretical and empirical base of this book, has been framed with the intention to understand the pattern of intercommunity interaction and the problems the Northeasterners face while living in India's metropolitan cities. Moving away from the attention generally given to factors of migration, the work seeks to document how cultural and racial minorities manage their life in a milieu where their identity is under constant interrogation and livelihood in a state of flux. It also tries to identify the mechanisms that small and predominantly rural-based communities employ to survive and maintain their community life in the flux and frenzy of the city while at the same time engage in intercommunity interactions.

This work also attempts to find out those factors and processes that have perpetuated violence and discriminatory practices towards the Northeasterners in Indian cities, by focusing on Delhi, their most preferred destination and India's Capital City. Popular discourse on Northeast tends to lay the blame for all forms of discrimination against Northeasterners at the doorstep of race. The study seeks to find out whether this is really the case, or are there other factors involved that have remained unnoticed to observers? Though race is generally defined in terms of biological characteristics, evidence reveals that racism as an ideology and practice feeds on the social and structural relations of the society within which it is embedded. This suggests that race is not a biological or naturally given entity *per se*, but a social construct that is shaped by the normative as well as the social structure within which it is embedded. Guided by this understanding, the book takes a hard look at the 'racial discrimination' thesis that dominates contemporary discourse on Northeast and emphasizes the need to isolate discriminations based on biological distinctions from those that are rooted in other structures of oppression prevalent in the society.

This demands that the analysis moves beyond specific incidents of violence to take into account the little acts of sharing and discord, which often take place at the personal level when people from different cultures and regions live and work together. Specific arenas of difference such as food habit as a site of cultural encounter and acts of sharing and points of conflict over food and social behaviour have been interrogated. Further, to gain an insight into the inner world of the Northeasterners, attitude towards marriage and/or intimate relations with the cultural 'other' within and beyond the Northeast have been analysed. This aspect can be considered as the ultimate form of personal action that can break the social boundaries or mark it out distinctly.

Though our primary interest has been the everyday experience and social encounters that take place between the Northeasterners and people of the city, we have also tried to examine how the state responds to the problem. In an era when the power of the state is intruding into every aspect of our life and the people too look up to the state for solution of their multifarious problems, it becomes imperative that we take a close look at how the state handles the situation. Ironically, it took the loss of several innocent lives and nation-wide protests against atrocities inflicted on Northeasterners to get the state to finally wake up and take note of the situation and not treat it as a routine law and order problem, as it has been wont to do. How effective is this response and how has the affected community react to it are some of the issues we have attempted to address in this book.

Methodology

Different tools of data collection have been employed to source the materials used in this book. In the first phase of the study, the data was primarily collected through the survey method, where questionnaires were distributed to select category of people identified for the purpose. To ensure that we get maximum information on the issues under investigation, attempts have been made to make the questions more analytical and extensive, rather than wholly focusing on the closed-ended options. For purpose of convenience, questionnaires were distributed to people hailing from the states of Manipur, Meghalaya and Nagaland. Data collection was initiated by taking the services of three field investigators: one each for the state of Manipur, Meghalaya and Nagaland. Questionnaires were distributed to 150 persons from the three Northeastern states living in the city; 50 for each state selected through snowball sampling. As the bulk of migrants from the Northeast comprised students and young white-collar professionals, majority of the respondents belong to these two categories, but cutting across ethnicity, language, religion and gender. Not all the questionnaires that were distributed to the prospective respondents however could be collected. Out of 150 sets of questionnaires distributed, we were able to get back only 129. There was difficulty in getting back all the questionnaires, as some respondents were not too responsive and others had left the city for some other destination. Although we were aware of the possibility that not all questionnaires handed out would be returned, we consciously opted for this tool because of the high privacy it offers to the respondents. As many of the issues dealt with are highly personal and intimate, the anonymity of the tool enhances the possibility of getting frank and honest answers. The kind of answers we received from many respondents reinforced our faith in the instrument.

In the second phase, where the focus shifted from the private world of respondents to the wider political domain the data was collected through direct observation, interviews and conversations with key persons in government establishments, civil society and cross sections of people in the homes and localities they reside. Some of the data was sourced from social networking sites in the Internet. For obvious reasons, a mix of the quantitative and qualitative method has been used in the analysis of the data. While demographic data has been collected and analysed quantitatively, qualitative method has been used to map and analyse information relating to experience, attitudes, opinions and feelings.

A major problem faced in the study and subsequent preparation of the book is the absence of a common nomenclature that is applicable to the diverse ethnic groups and communities of Northeast. Numbering more than 200 distinct communities, with their own language, customs and culture, each community is known by its ethnic or tribal identity making the task of defining them collectively highly problematic.[3] In the absence of a common name and lack of more suitable equivalents, we were forced to settle for the rather prosaic and matter-of-fact word 'Northeasterner' to refer to the people of the Northeastern states as a whole irrespective of their socio-cultural background or state to which they belong. Although the root word, 'Northeast' from which the name 'Northeasterner' is derived, carries a geographical connotation, there is nothing local about its origin. Rather, as the medium suggests, the concept is a colonial legacy born of the British administration's expansionist policy and 'frontier' making in early nineteenth century. Today, the name Northeast has been internalized both by the Indian state and by the concerned population.[4]

On the converse, the terms 'mainstream' and 'mainlander' have been used to refer to the majority community and those in prominence in the country. While it is difficult to construe the 'mainstream' or 'mainlander' as specific categories in terms of sharing common characteristics exclusive to themselves, we have opted for these terms because this is how Northeasterners refer to India's dominant population in their daily conversations and cognitive understanding. In certain instances, the term 'local' population has been used to refer to the dominant population in the localities where the Northeasterners reside in the city.

Another problem faced in the study is the absence of records on the number of persons from Northeast studying, working or living in Delhi. According to the report published by North East Support Centre & Helpline (NESCH, 2011), there are more than two lakh persons from the Northeastern states who live in the capital. There is however no documentary evidence to authenticate the information or to get accurate estimates of those currently in residence in the city. Inquiries made with various agencies, including Ministry of Development of North Eastern Region (MoDONER) and State Guest Houses or Bhawans, yielded little success. From the latter, only piecemeal and disparate information could be obtained from the registration books on guests who halted at the Bhawan(s), with no proper record on the number of people, purpose of visit or length of stay in the city. Similar is the case with records maintained by students and religious organizations, many of which comprised names of persons constantly on the move. Hence while there is visibly a large presence of Northeasterners in Delhi, the exact number is shrouded in ambiguity. The same is true of other metros in the country.

Outline of the Study

The book opens with the examination of the theoretical underpinnings and conceptual discourse on people of Northeast as the cultural and racial 'other'. Taking a cue from contemporary discourse on the problems faced by Northeasterners in cities across India, those issues that have been widely debated in public and private platforms have been interrogated further. The chapter also spells out the themes, objectives and methodology employed to source the materials used in the book.

This is followed by a brief account of the political history of Northeast India, by way of examining the etymology of the concept 'Northeasterner', which constitutes the subject of our discussion. Further, extending the discussion on Northeasterners as the social and cultural 'other', initiated in the Introduction, the chapter takes a close look at the process and politics of 'othering'/'otherness' by simultaneously drawing on the works of prominent scholars in the discipline and examples from the field to locate the social and cultural position of being a 'Northeasterner' in India's metropolitan city, a place that is not only physically far away from 'home' but also underlined by values and ethos that are often alien to the people and society of Northeast. On the conceptual plane, those criteria that have been generally employed to mark people from Northeast have been identified and analysed to bring out how different cultural origin can affect intergroup relations.

Chapter 3 presents the social and economic profile of the respondents, focusing in particular on their occupation, modes of migration, place of origin and the means they employed while moving to the city. Further, to understand the conditions under which Northeasterners live in the city, attempts are made to find out the problems and challenges they experienced in getting a place to stay in the city. As part of the analysis, we have looked at the types of residential accommodation that the respondents reside in and whose services they have obtained while getting the accommodation. Relations with the landlords and the terms and conditions laid down by them have also been examined. Attempts are also made to ascertain whether people from Northeast prefer to stay in areas generally populated by members of their own community or seek other options offering better facilities and personal conveniences away from their own kind. This aspect has been examined to ascertain whether 'ghetto' culture exists among the Northeasterners in terms of residential preference.

Given that the sense of community is generally realized through active participation in the community activities, we have also tried to map the community activities that the people from Northeast normally engaged in during their stay in the city. Beginning with their regular church activities, we have tried to analyse the Northeasterners' response to community activities, role of students' organizations and allied bodies. Aspects of positive and negative orientations towards intercommunity relations have also been looked at.

Chapter 4 takes on the vexed question of racial discrimination that is popularly considered as a major problem that Northeasterners encounter in the cities they migrate. In order to identify the actual discriminations experienced, we have looked into the Northeasterners' dressing style, food habits and physical movement while living in the city. Also, the forms and accounts of actual atrocities experienced have been taken into consideration while looking into the problems of social discrimination. Apart from data generated through the survey and personal interviews, recent incidents that shot into prominence through media reports and public debates have also been examined and incorporated in the discussion.

Moving on to more intimate areas of social and cultural encounters, attempts have been made to understand the social dynamics at the work place. Brief profile of Northeast workers in Delhi region has been analysed, focusing both on the difficulties they encounter in the environment and the relations they forged with their peers. Viewing food as a powerful tool that can narrow the distance between groups, sharing of food among the colleagues in the office has been examined to understand the dynamics of cross-cultural relations through food exchange as well as the acts of sharing and social acceptance that take place between persons in close groups.

Chapter 5 turns its attention on the contentious issue of cross-cultural marriage. Given that marriage is an important element that marks the boundary between groups, attempt has been made to find out whether migration to distant places influences the manner in which Northerners choose their life partners. To elicit the information and assess their openness or otherwise towards marriage and intimate relations with the social and cultural 'other', their opinion on interethnic and interreligious marriage and friendship with the opposite gender outside the community has been examined. This has been done with an attempt to understand the aspects of defining the social and cultural 'other' from within and without.

Next, moving from the intimate world of marriage and sexuality into the wider political domain, attempts are made to examine how the state responds to what is generally called the 'Northeast problem'. Among other things, this involved taking a close and critical look at the Bezbaruah Committee, set up by the Central Government in 2014 to address the growing violence against the people of Northeast in the Indian cities, the recommendations it came up with and their implementation by different organs of the government. This was by no means an easy task. The contemporariness of the issue meant that we had to engage in continuous fieldwork that involved, among other things, participation in meetings and constant contact with persons in key positions to ascertain the facts, besides keeping tab on official websites and social media to keep up with developments that lie beyond the reach of the conventional model of fieldwork. As a corollary, attempts have also been made to map the response of civil society and Northeast community to the process and what mechanisms they employ to cope with and adapt to the situation. The findings are revealing. The analysis reveals that there is a distinct paradigm shift not only in the Northeasterner's approach to the problem but also in the discourse: moving from the language of discrimination and victimhood, that informs popular discourse, to citizenship and participation.

The issues discussed in the chapter and the procedures involved in sourcing the materials from the field lent a distinctive quality to the text where the authors have been pushed to don the cap of *researchers* and the *researched* at one and at the same time. Though our disciplinary training had forewarned us to be wary of letting our subjectivities come in the way we see and interpret the facts, we would be dishonest to our profession if we do not acknowledge that our personal location helped us, in no small way, not only to access but also to make sense of the materials used. We leave it to the readers to judge whether we had erred in this.

Finally, the concluding chapter revisits some of the key issues discussed earlier in the text. Questions were also raised and new areas for policy and research identified for action by policy makers and future scholars interested in the subject.

In short, the questions raised in the book and our overall engagement with this work has been driven by the imperative to understand how the Northeasterners, as the social and cultural 'other' survive in a milieu where not only their identity but also their nationality have been questioned at every turn.

Notes

1. According to the 2011 census, less than one-third (27.70%) of the population of Northeast is made up of Scheduled Tribes.
2. Discrimination and Challenges before Women from North East India: Case Studies from Four Metros: New Delhi, Mumbai, Kolkata and Bengaluru, A Study conducted by Centre for North East Studies and Policy Research, Jamia Millia Islamia, New Delhi, 2014.

3. In terms of linguistic diversity alone, out of 1652 spoken languages in India 325 are in Northeast (K.S. Singh and S. Manoharan, *Peoples of India,* Vol. IX, Oxford University Press, 1994); see also *Encyclopedia of North-East India,* Volume I by Col Ved Prakash, Delhi, Atlantic, 2007, and George van Driem, 2012. 'Glimpses of the Ethnolinguistic Prehistory of North-eastern India' in Toni Huber and Stuart Blackburn (eds), *Origins and Migrations in the Extended Eastern Himalayas.* Leiden: Brill, pp. 187–211.
4. For more on this, see Chapter 2.

CHAPTER 2

Locating Northeasterners in Delhi

While trying to locate Northeasterners in the city, it is important to recognize that people from Northeast India are not homogenous in their origin, beliefs, culture and ethnic identity. Not only do the people from this region come from separate states, they also have varied cultural identities and ethnic affiliations. Many have also had a long tradition of resistance pitted against the Indian state to thwart its control over their territories. For instance, some sections of the Naga, Meitei and Bodo ethnic communities continue to be engaged in active movements for establishing their own sovereign states. Notwithstanding the vast diversity within, people from Northeast have generally been viewed as a singular entity with common ethos and way of life, both by the state and people in general. What we witnessed is continuous construction of 'Northeasterners' as an undifferentiated group of people characterized by common features of race, beliefs and lifestyles that are not only different from the rest of India, but also stand in sharp contrast to the dominant culture of the country. Further, over emphasis on Northeasterners as a group of people located within a specific geographical space within the map of a nation has led to construction of people's identity solely on the basis of geography, ignoring the internal variation that divides the region along lines of ethnicity, language, beliefs and practices.

Decoding Northeast India: Historical Roots and Making of the 'Other'

To place things in their proper social and political perspectives, it would be instructive to examine the concept 'Northeast' from which the nomenclature 'Northeasterner' used in this discussion is derived. As a concept, 'Northeast' came into existence during the colonial period to refer to the large tracts of land sandwiched between Bengal in the South West and Burma in the East. Initially, the area was described as the 'Eastern' (Pemberton, 1935)[1] and later as the 'North-eastern frontier' (Mackenzie, 1882)[2] of British India (for details see Bhaumik, 2010).[3] As a 'frontier', the Northeast was seen to lie not only outside the pale of civilization distinct from British administered India, but also an area to be administered and controlled by varied means, depending upon the perception and needs of the empire. However, the mode in which the entity 'Northeast' has been imagined over the years has undergone series of transformations. From what was originally conceived as a 'frontier' of the British Empire, the Northeast has metamorphosed into a 'region' with a distinct identity within independent India's nation-state. What stands out in the conceptualization of Northeast India as a region is the emphasis placed on its oneness, a fact that finds vivid reflection in the use of the biological metaphor 'seven sisters' to refer to the seven states, namely, Arunachal Pradesh, Assam, Manipur, Meghalaya, Mizoram, Nagaland and Tripura, that make up the entity – now eight sisters, with the addition of Sikkim in 1972. In more recent times, following India's new foreign policy initiative to forge closer economic ties with the ASEAN countries post-liberalization, Northeast has been described as the 'bridgehead' that connects the Indian subcontinent to South, Southeast and East Asia. Its strategic geo-political location with 98 per cent of its borders linked to five sovereign states – Bhutan, China and Nepal in the north, Bangladesh in the west and Myanmar in the east and south. Northeast has been seen as an ideal site to take the Indian government's ambitious 'Look East' (GOI, 2008)[4], or its current avatar 'Act East' policy forward.

Alongside the changes in the nomenclature and the perceived relevance of the region to national policy, much transformation has also taken place within the region in the intervening post-independence period. The colonially driven Christianization process, re-organization of states and spates of ethnic movement post-independence have given rise to complex and, at the same time, contradictory processes of fragmentation, and alignments and re-alignments of groups across the communities in Northeast. All of these factors play a vital role in shaping the relations of the people of Northeast with the Indian state, on the one hand, and fellow citizens from other parts of the country, on the other hand.

The perception of mainland India towards the Northeasterners and vice versa has long been a contested affair. On the one hand, people from the Northeast region have felt neglected and discriminated against by the state and mainland population. On the contrary, the Indian state and people of the mainland have been wont to view the Northeasterner as not only culturally and racially different but also quite distant to the idea of India in terms of their perception and sense of belongingness, a fact mainlanders contend is illustrated by the radical ideologies and violent conflicts perpetrated by rebel groups and 'insurgents' from Northeast against the Indian state. The fact that majority of the Northeasterners are wary of the 'rebels', and the fact that Northeast as a political entity constitutes an integral part of the Indian Union bound by a common constitution and administrative machinery, proved inadequate to bridge the social and psychological gulf that underlined the relations between the peoples of Northeast and mainland India. Hence, what we find in this gamut of cultural and social disjunction is numerous manifestations of constructing a stereotypical image of diverse groups of people, where monolithic features such as race, culture and religion are played out to create a divergent 'other'.

Many scholars from the region have argued that in India, there is something that constitutes the 'mainstream', which fundamentally excludes the 'Northeast' as the 'other' (see in particular Akoijam, 2012). According to the author, this construction of Northeast as the 'other', though based on 'geographical criterion', has a lot to do with 'racial', cultural and political criteria (ibid.). This not only begs the question 'what constitutes the other' but also calls for close scrutiny of the process of *othering*.

In Western discourse, the cultural 'other' is generally perceived to occupy a position that is backward in time and lacks the progress that characterizes developed societies. The 'other' in such context may not actually be the recognition of difference, but an epistemological construction, which may be based on the ethnographer's knowledge or preconceived ideas of the issue or entity at hand (Sarukkai, 1997). In the recent past, the construction of the 'other' has emerged on varied grounds: social, cultural and also geographical, as in the case of the 'East'–'West' distinction that pervades colonial writings. The representation of the eastern world as the 'other' in the writings of nineteenth-century Europe, as Edward Said has argued, was not based on actual facts on the ground, but on preconceived archetypes that envision all 'Eastern' (read 'non-Western') societies as similar to one another, and fundamentally different to 'Western' societies (Said, 1978).

Construction of the 'other' may have emerged in various societies by emphasizing on points of difference between societies; however, the problem may lie in comprehending the dissimilarities. The 'other' can be found or invented in any social and cultural context, where religious, social and racial boundaries and diversities exist. As a highly heterogeneous country, India has numerous social and cultural boundaries, producing layers of 'others', such as, Dalit, tribes, religious minorities (viz. Christians, Muslims, Parsis and so on) and women, with the 'Northeasterner' as the latest entrant in the list. With poor development and employment opportunities forcing the people to look for survival outside the region, people from Northeast India are emerging as the conspicuous 'other' in cities across India. What is also highly significant is the fact that the Northeasterner is being marked out not only as 'different', but also as 'ill-fitted' in the social and cultural map of predominantly Aryan India.

It would be erroneous to assume that 'othering' is a unilateral process, but mutually constituted, universally. The distinction between 'we' and 'they' is a widely pervasive human feature found across cultures, in which people of one's own are defined differently from the other(s). This by itself is not a negative thing. What makes it so is the importation of value judgment in the construction and the tendency to view the 'other' as inferior to or less worthy than the 'self'. This tendency has made othering a highly vitiated issue and a major source of conflict between groups across the social and cultural spectrum.

Viewed thus, an important question that arises is, how has the conceptualization of the Northeasterner as the 'other' affected their daily life in the cities they migrate. The city has its own social dynamics where construction of the 'other' will also be within the context of the local social situation. Hence, the impact of such construction on their experience of everyday life in the city needs to be interrogated. Whether the political conflicts that had perpetually besieged the Northeast after India's independence could have any impact on the people's personal interactions in the city is one of the aspects that we need to probe. On the one hand, there have been instances where Northeasterners who have experienced traumatic situations back home in their relations with the state and its law enforcing agencies have not been able to come to terms with 'mainstream' India. On the other, we have locals who are not able to locate people from Northeast as fellow citizens of the country. It is the encounter of this divergent group of individuals that is changing the social contours of urban India. Some social encounters have turned into cordial relationship and created hybrid cultural and social compositions; while in others it has led to deep acrimony.

Cities and Citizenship: Challenging the Idea of Cohesive Society

More than conceiving the problems of people from Northeast in mainland cities as stray incidents that concern only the life of migrants who have chosen to move out of their home state for work and education in the city, it would be more pertinent to consider the problem as one that pertains to rights of citizenships and idea of the nation. As Arjun Appadurai and James Holston have argued:

> Although one of the essential projects of nation building has been to dismantle the historic primacy of urban citizenship and to replace it with the national, cities remain the strategic arena for the development of citizenship. (1996: 188)

Going further, they wrote:

> But with their concentrations of the nonlocal, the strange, the mixed, and the public, cities engaged most palpably the tumult of citizenship. Their streets conflate identities of territory and contract with those of race, religion, class, culture, and gender to produce reactive ingredients of both progressive and reactionary political movements. Like nothing else, the modern urban public signifies both the defamiliarizing enormity of national citizenship and exhilaration of its liberties. (1996: 188)

Cities are just not sites of conflict and intermixing, but also the arena where the actual political idea of citizenship is tested and challenged. Therefore, the forms and nature of interaction or accommodation between the native dwellers of the city and the migrant population, or between the diverse ethnic groups who have moved to the city take place at the political field as well.

It would therefore not be inapt to relate the problems that social and cultural minorities face in the cities to their rights of national citizenship. This is particularly necessary when that group of minorities happen to be non-local and of different racial stock from the dominant population. This being the case, they may be considered 'strange' by some local inhabitants who have been living in the city for several generations before the migrants arrive. Not only the social and political origin of the migrant minority, but also the historical conjecture of the city, shapes the idea of citizenship in the city. The arrival of the Northeasterner in Delhi is a case in point where the Northeast 'other' is not only nonlocal in origin but also different in several socio-cultural aspects, including race. Hence, their attempts to carve out a niche for themselves in the city can invite different forms of resistance and contestations, including their nationality, from the city dweller. What is more, where resources are scarce and the competition intense, the relation can take an ugly turn.

Delhi as one of the early mega-polis and capital of the country has been taking the brunt of migration-linked population expansion. While describing Delhi as a form of 'mongrel city', Ayona Datta traces that trajectory of Delhi accepting the 'other' in the violent past of India's Partition and militancy in other parts of the country (Datta, 2011: 750). Since 1947, when people from across the newly created international border came to settle down in Delhi, varied communities from different parts of India have moved to the city seeking refuge and better livelihood opportunities (ibid). Delhi has accommodated Punjabis, Sikhs, Bengalis and Kashmiri Hindus, who moved to the city in search of security from violent situations. From the 1950s, Delhi has also experienced large influx of migrants from the rural areas to escape the scourge of poverty and landlessness. Further, post-1991, which marked the onset of India's economic liberalization, people from Northeast India have steadily moved to Delhi and other cities in search of better education and employment opportunities. Most of the migrants to the city have ended up sharing the same locality living as close door neighbours, in the process began to learn about the 'other' through intimate mixing not just in the public sphere but personally as well.

Contributing to the mix is the dearth of housing to accommodate the continuous flow of migrants into the city, forcing the new arrivals to look for accommodation amongst the local population in congested localities. While India's political leaders have repeatedly proclaimed their promise to make Delhi a world-class city in every aspect, in real terms the city is highly deficient in facilities to cater to the needs of the growing population. While infrastructures have been developed to accommodate the demands of rising economic growth and global trade, there has also been simultaneous exclusion of the poor from this dream project (Dupoint, 2011). The global city model of housing patterns has not been designed to meet the needs of the poor and the ever-increasing migrants in the city, whose presence is critical to meet the rising demand for labour and other professional services in different sectors of the global economy. It is in this context that we find migrants from diverse parts of the country are pushed to the fringe of the metropolis to live in the old city villages, which have gradually metamorphosed into urban localities.

The presence of the 'other' became more pertinent when the shared space and lived experiences became more intimate and close. For the Northeasterners, this has often ended up in placing them at the receiving end of cultural and racial stereotypes from locals in the city. But as long as peace prevails, with locals and migrants living side by side without much conundrum, there is little need for the state to interfere. But when conflict escalates and peace is disrupted, state intervention becomes a necessity and protecting the lives of citizens, irrespective of their origin, becomes imperative. It is in such tumultuous situations that the feeling of 'otherness' and presence of the 'other' become not just abstract constructions, but also a problem that needs to be resolved. A case in point is the conflict that erupted between the landlords and Northeast migrants in Munirka in February 2014 when the local police had to be called to restcre peace in the locality. Though localized in nature, the incident has emerged as a vital example where the Northeasterners' right to space and citizenship has been seriously challenged by the host society.

Munirka, a Jat village in South Delhi, is a popular locality for students and young professionals by virtue of its proximity to the Indira Gandhi International Airport and premier institutions such as Jawaharlal Nehru University (JNU), National Institute of Health and Family Welfare, the Indian Institute of Technology (IIT) and allied institutions, backed by easy availability of accommodation specially built by the land-rich locals for rent. Sensing the economic prospects of owning property for lease, many landowners in the village have constructed multi-storied buildings, each housing dozens of apartments for lease to the ever-increasing migrant population. Aiding the construction boom is the special status of the village land. Categorized as *lal dora* land in the city's land revenue system, Munirka falls outside the jurisdiction of the Delhi Development Authority (DDA) and New Delhi Municipal Corporation (NDMC), the city's authorized agency that regulates and sanctions house and building construction in the capital city. This exclusion provides full 'freedom' to the landowners to construct houses with impunity. The net effect is that while Munirka offers affordable homes to the increasing flow of people from the Northeastern region, the host society steeped in caste and religious orthodoxy and patriarchal ideology find the Northeast tenants too different and bohemian for their liking. Though the economic benefits that accrue from the presence of migrants in the locality, in the form of rent from the leased out premises (which is generally charged at a much higher rate to the Northeasterner than they charged to others) and earnings from shops and other services they patronized had kept the tension under wraps, escalation in the feeling of 'otherness' by the increasing presence of the cultural 'other' and racial prejudice disrupted the tenuous peace in the relations between the locals and the migrants.

On 17 February 2014, news spread among the Northeast residents that the Panchayat of Munirka had passed a resolution to evict all Northeast tenants as they found them a 'bad influence' on the locals. This prompted Northeast activists to approach the Delhi Police to intervene and stop the Panchayat from executing the resolution. After series of meetings and negotiations between Northeast representatives, the local police and village authorities at the Vasant Vihar police station, truce was arrived at. While the Village Authority (Panchayat) flatly denied the passing of any resolution to evict the Northeast tenants, the news doing the round in the village was that the tenants should be in their apartments not later than 11 PM and no one should be found on the streets beyond that hour. Also, CCTV cameras would be installed in the streets to track 'anti-social' activities by the residents.

Close examination of the situation reveals that at the root of the matter lies the deep social and cultural gulf that characterized the relations between the migrants and the local inhabitants. In the first place, the landlords were deeply perturbed at the behaviour of the Northeasterners who unlike the local residents kept 'irregular' hours coming in and out of their homes at 'odd hours' of the day, a matter that is viewed with serious misgivings by the local community. What added to the problem was the fact that many of the Northeasterners residing in the locality work in BPOs and other service sectors, which follow working hours that conform to the timing of the firm's home country whose day time coincides with night in India. Hence, adhering to the curfew stipulated by the Panchayat could seriously compromise their livelihood. This is not the case with BPO workers alone. Even those working in India-based industry such as hotels, restaurants and tourism maintain working hours very different from those in government-run establishments. The same applies to contractual workers in state-run institutions. Some women who work in the state *Bhawans* on a shift basis, which often includes staying back late at work, especially during visits of state dignitaries and senior officials, claim that the proposed curfew by the village authority has exposed them to unnecessary harassments and questioning by landlords.

Northeasterners have also found themselves caught in the conflicting expectations of the workplace and the locality they live in with respect to clothes and fashion. With many of the workplaces switching over to international standards in matters of dress and appearance of their employees to keep up with the demands of the age of globalization, the donning of Western attire by the Northeast female are often construed by the locals as an indication of their loose moral character with little respect to modesty and tradition. It is significant that this perception is at sharp variance with the views of persons in industry, who see the Northeasterner's oriental looks, mode of dressing, proficiency in English and accent, as requisites that significantly add to the global image of the firm they work in. Indeed, many entrepreneurs in aviation, hospitality and beauty industry have praised the Northeast youths for their smartness, articulation and dedication to their work. Seen as disciplined and honest workers, they are in high demand in departmental stores, beauty parlours, spas, health care clinics, hospitals, hotels, restaurants and sundry others. Interestingly, while these qualities have positively added to the employment prospects of the Northeasterners, the same have contributed to their discrimination and accusations of being un-Indian by the local population. In an interview given to the *Times of India* on the issue of hostility expressed towards Northeast migrants, entrepreneur C. Balagopal and former Indian Administrative Service (IAS) officer states: '... [S]ome hostility has come into prominence recently due to large numbers finding employment in cities across India. Their smart looks, Westernized dress and informal approach make them successful in vocations like hospitality and travel – that's a reason for adverse attention' (*TOI*, 2014).[5]

It is not the employed alone who found themselves pitted against the local normative structure. Equally affected are the students. In apparent oblivion of the cultural ethos of the host society, where the behaviour and movements of the youth are under the strict lens of the family, the gregarious nature and free and easy ways of the Northeast youths have brought them into serious conflict with their landlords and neighbours. Their fondness for loud songs and music and tendency to flock together, irrespective of sex, are some of the behaviours considered most objectionable. Embedded in a milieu where generation hierarchy and segregation of the sexes are undisputed norms, homeowners view the Northeasterner's easy-going behaviour as a serious threat to their staid and age-old tradition.

To arrive at a meaningful understanding of the situation, it would be useful to focus our attention on some of the cultural practices prevailing in the Northeastern region, which exert an influence on the behaviour of the youth. Prominent among these is the bachelor's dormitory where adolescents and youths stay together away from the family to engage in various activities. Though the name and form vary, the bachelors' dormitory is a vital institution prevalent among many tribes. It is a socialization agency par excellence where the seniors acculturate the juniors in the norms and values of the society and impart various skills, ranging from sports and storytelling to training in agriculture and warfare. The dormitory not only serves as an important source of labour with a ready workforce to render service to families in need, but also as a relief and rescue team in any emergency that may arise in the community.

Writing on the Morung, the bachelor's dormitory of the Nagas, Kamaladevi Chattopadhyay notes:

> The younger boys learn to serve the older ones, assume tasks to serve the morung, roughing out in a group, moulding them to make difficult adjustments. The tougher elements are hammered into moderation for, otherwise, they are open to chastisement and ridicule. For bad behavior, a severe punishment may also be given. The training also reduces the tension between the old and younger generation, In short, fulfilling a variety of functions. It is a kind of a club for the young people where they learn to sing community songs, dancing, ornamentation, decoration. (Chattopadhyay, 1978: 83; see also Bareh, 1970: 84–85)[6]

Though the dormitory is an institution of the past, the principles that gave birth to it and the social and cultural values it nurtures through collective action continue to exert a strong influence in the life of Northeast youths. Exposure to education and the forces of modernization and change has eroded the physical aspect of the dormitory. However, the social ethos and co-operative spirit associated with it continue to be alive and have travelled with the people wherever they go. Hence what the landlords view as excessive gregarious behaviour displayed by Northeast youths in the city is nothing but a re-enactment of a way of life they have been used to, albeit in new forms. Though separated from their homeland, and living amidst people of diverse races and cultures, nostalgia and a sense of duty keep majority of Northeasterners close to their tradition, and to each other.

Casual conversations carried out with members of the local community reveal that many are ignorant of the culture and tradition of the migrants. Unfamiliar with the Northeasterners' customary practices and the value they attach to community, and the importance of keeping their cultural traditions alive through collective action, many view their behaviour as 'outlandish' and 'un-becoming' of Indians, hence they need to be *corrected*.

It would be instructive to recall the views of the locals we spoke to on the matter: Asha, whose father-in-law owns an apartment block that is rented out to Northeast tenants and has a fourteen years old son, is worried that the Northeasterner's Western lifestyle and fashion will corrupt her son. Geeta who works as a domestic help for middle class families in the adjacent DDA complex, wants her teenage daughter to acquire a good education like students of JNU but fears her character would be ruined if she interacts with girls from Northeast whose way of dressing and friendship with the boys she considers highly improper. Rameshwar a shop assistant in the village market finds nothing wrong with the Northeast families residing in the locality, but is critical of the youth, who he claims have ruined the locality by their irregular hours and rowdy songs and music, '*yeh log mohalla barbad kardya*' (these people have destroyed the locality) he rued. An interesting comment on the issue comes from a local autorickshaw driver who has ferried and seen many Northeast youths from close quarters. Reminiscent of the view made by Delhi Police in their booklet of instructions to Northeasterners in Delhi, he states, '*in logo ki rivaaz hamare se alag hai, videshi lagta hai, lekin agar in koh Delhi me rahane hai toh hamare bhavnao ka samaan karana chahiye*' (these people's customs are different from ours, they are like foreigners, but if they want to live in Delhi they should respect our sentiments). He supports the *diktat* issued by the village authorities to regulate their movement.

Many Northeasterners expressed concern at the manner in which the local community views the situation. Many claim that while they have been placed under a blanket of suspicion, the hosts exhibit utter indifference to crimes committed against them. Not long before the eviction controversy erupted, a Northeast girl was raped and murdered by an IIT student who lived next to her brother's apartment in which the crime was committed. Another girl was allegedly raped by the landlord's son and was forced to leave the place in fear and humiliation. Commenting on the incidents, a woman from Meghalaya rued,

> [N]o one is bothered when it does not happen to one's own. There is little respect for human life in general. People may get beaten up and die at your doorstep, it is none of your business if that person is not related to you. This indifference is characteristic of both landlords and tenants. So life goes on under the guise of normalcy, but the rot cannot be stopped, it seeps deep into the psyche and flares up at the least provocation.

This sad observation and the comments detailed in the foregoing paragraph not only vividly mirror the otherness of the Northeasterners in the city they reside, but also raised serious questions about their rights as citizens

Generalizing the 'Other': Construction of Northeasterners as a Distinct Group

Some forms of expressions that indicate the distinction between communities living in the periphery and centre have shot into prominence in the recent years. As seen in the context of the present discussion, terms such as 'mainstream' and 'other' have entered the scene in a major way, both in ordinary conversations and in academic discourse. While the 'other' which denotes people who are socially and culturally different from the 'self' has had a long history in the social sciences, the term 'mainstream' is of more recent origin. People from Northeast have routinely resorted to usage of the term 'mainstream' while referring to the majority community and those in prominence in the country. However, it is difficult to construe the 'mainstream' as a specific category in terms of sharing common characteristics exclusive to itself, rather the concept is understood in general terms as the 'dominant' community or culture and those enjoying state power and authority over affairs of the country. In the same manner, the term 'Northeast' has been generalized in terms of not only belonging to a specific geographical area but also constituting a 'community', such as 'tribe' or 'Christians', and a particular race (primarily of Mongolian stock). In this characterization, the diversity of the people of Northeast with respect to their ethnicity, language and historical experience has received little attention. On the contrary, as one scholar notes, '[T]here is frequent generalization of the northeastern region in terms of race, topography and as a troubled periphery with multifarious law and order problems' (Haokip, 2012: 84–85). Compounded by numerous problems that besieged the region, people of Northeast do find themselves in similar situational predicament, whether they are at home or away from it. But the most common and overt way of categorizing the Northeasterner is as people belonging to 'Mongoloid' family and defined as such by the use of the pejorative term 'chinky' or slit-eyes. This characterization is not only found among laymen, but also extensively used by intellectuals and administrators alike while interrogating the contours of Northeast.

The problem with the above characterization comes out sharply when we relate it to the demographic structure of the region. In demographic terms, India's Northeast comprises vastly heterogeneous categories of people belonging to different ethnic, linguistic and racial stocks. While the population in the states of Arunachal Pradesh, Manipur, Meghalaya, Mizoram and Nagaland is predominantly of Mongoloid stock, the inhabitants of Assam and Tripura are mainly of Caucasoid stock with a sizable segment belonging to the Negroid family, with different degrees of acculturation and assimilation with the dominant population. As per the 2011 Census, 27.70 per cent of the population of Northeast belongs to the category of Scheduled Tribes, showing a marginal increase over the 2001 Census, which stood at 26.9 per cent (see Annexure 1 for distribution among states). This implies that more than two-thirds of the Northeast population comprised non-tribes. Interestingly, notwithstanding the large presence of non-tribes in the region, people from Northeast have generally been considered to be of tribal origin, or having the features of tribes in their lifestyle and culture. What makes the generalization more problematic is the underlying idea that Northeasterners are not only socially and culturally different from the dominant communities in the metropolitan cities, but also occupy a lower position in the social hierarchy.

In the recent events that have taken place where problems faced by people from Northeast residing in cities in mainland India have gained wide media coverage and state attention, some scholars have argued that some kind of pan-Northeast solidarity has emerged among the migrants from the region (see in particular McDuie-Ra, 2012b: 69–77). The author supports this contention by citing the case of coming together of diverse ethnic groups from Northeast sinking their deep rooted differences to collectively protest against the continuing imposition of the draconian Armed Forces Special Powers Act, 1958 (AFSPA) in some states in the region. The configuration of strengthened Northeast solidarity in the wake of atrocities against them in cities across the mainland is undeniably a new form of identity formation. However, it needs to be recognized that this reconfiguration of Northeast identity has little link with shared history or culture of the people; neither does it have correlations with the dynamics of identity politics prevalent 'back home' in the Northeastern region, which is underlined by divergence rather than confluence of interests. Hence the pan-Northeast solidarity referred to is shaped not by having shared experience within the region, but by the status of being migrants in the metro cities and belonging to a specific region or space. Viewed thus, belongingness to a specific geographical space and the meaning imputed to the status by those external to it has emerged as the common denominator for the Northeasterners in India's metropolitan cities and towns where they find themselves as migrants. However, to what extent this solidarity is translated into a durable element that transcends the primordial divide based on caste, tribe and ethnicity requires close scrutiny.

Extensive categorization of Northeast as a distinct entity with common characteristics amidst the cauldron of divergent identities, the common identity concept imposed upon them have gradually been internalized by the Northeasterners themselves. Situational crisis and circumstances that have made Northeasterners as the 'other' in cities have invariably produced certain forms of cohesion within the community. However, the critical question that arises is whether this feeling of solidarity/cohesion can be translated into a durable element that transcends the primordial divide rooted in caste, tribe and ethnicity. Our investigations yield no conclusive data on this score. The findings suggest the process is still in an incipient stage and is yet to be translated into a strengthened bond of social and political alignments among the Northeasterners back in the region or in the cities where they have come to stay. It would be interesting to see how this process shapes up in the long run.

The Racialized 'Other': Physical Difference as Cumulative Social Identity

What makes people from Northeast a distinct group and their experiences of living in the city different from people belonging to other regions? According to some scholars who have delved on the issue, the answer to this query can be found in 'race'. In the words of McDuie-Ra, 'India contains many communities marked as 'others', based on religion, caste and even ethnicity, yet the nationality and origin of these people are not questioned at every turn' (2012b). This is because, the author avers, most of the communities can easily 'blend in' with the heartland, while Northeast migrants could not due to their distinctive looks and life ways. Though every community suffers from some form of discrimination, Northeast migrants' experience of racism is distinct in many ways from those experienced by others. The Northeasterner is not only labelled as 'chinky', an unflattering term directed at their Mongoloid features of small eyes and snub nose, doubts have also been cast on their nationality and very identity as Indians by conflating them with the Chinese, the Nepalis and the Tibetans, people who are primarily of foreign nationality.

Discussions held with key informants and cross sections of Northeast students disclosed that their identity as Indians has frequently been put to the test by the country's law enforcing agency, the city police and security guards (both government and private), who routinely demanded persons from the region to produce their passport or ID card as proof of their identity. The doubt that surrounds their identity even finds its echo in the perspective of national political parties. Giving fuel to its opponents to hit out at the party, the Bharatiya Janata Party (BJP), India's largest political party which currently runs the government at the Centre in its Election Manifesto released in the run up to the Delhi Legislative Assembly election on 7 February 2015, described the people of Northeast India as 'immigrants', that is people who have come to live permanently in a foreign country, thereby implying that they are aliens or foreigners in their homeland and country of birth. When Northeast activists and the mass media questioned the description, the party was quick to issue an explanation and attributed the *faux pas* to a typographical error stating that it actually meant migrants.[7] Many, however, were not convinced and view the statement as a Freudian slip.

Close observation of the situation shows that people from Northeast, although sharply aware of their distinct physical appearance, rarely imagined or presented themselves in terms of race. Rather, they present themselves on the basis of their ethnic identity; this happens both in the states back home and in the towns and cities they migrate to. Most of the Northeast associations and institutions are set up on the lines of tribe and ethnicity.[8] Race as a marker of their collective identity is a relatively new phenomenon that is superimposed upon them in the midst of growing violence they experience in the city. The feeling of being racially different has only come when they migrate and live in the mainland cities and identified as such by the host society. In fact, till the time we began this study, we found no data that suggest Northeasterners ever come together on the basis of race; rather it is the region that has united them in times of crisis.

However, the spate of violence that people of Northeast have experienced in the cities in recent times has forced a turn in the way in which Northeasterners look at the problem and the strategies they adopted to deal with the situation. Moving away from their traditional reluctance to come together under the banner of race, in February 2014 a group of Northeast activists, professionals and students got together to set up the 'North East India Forum Against Racism' (NEIFAR) to fight against the malaise and to lobby with the government and those in positions of power for introduction of a law that would criminalize discrimination of persons on the basis of race. What triggered the formation of NEIFAR is the absence of a law that could try offenders against a Northeasterner under the label of racist crime, in line with obligations enforced on signatory states by the International Convention on Elimination of Racial Discrimination. The urgency for such a law was triggered by the combined effect of the Munirka incident, where cultural prejudice and a climate of suspicion have put the security and livelihood of Northeasterners at serious risks, and the refusal of Delhi Police to treat the death of Nido Tania as a racist attack. The ill fated 20 years old youth from Arunachal Pradesh was brutally beaten up by a group of shop keepers at the popular Lajpat Nagar market in South Delhi when he angrily responded to their taunt on his 'peculiar' hairstyle, resulting in his death a day later from injuries received during the beating. The circumstances leading to Tania's death and the general apathy exhibited towards violence perpetrated on people of Northeast origin was the proverbial last straw that forced the Northeast activists to rally together under the banner of race, to fight for a law they perceived would enable them to live in safety and with dignity in the towns and cities they have made their home away from home.[9]

Implicit in the process outlined above is the fact that whereas race may have emerged as an important element in the construction of the Northeast identity, it is an externally imposed identity that is traditionally alien to the people's imagination of themselves. Even when race is used as a rallying point to mobilize the people for collective action, as borne out by the establishment of NEIFAR noted above, it does not signify common identity or shared ideology at the level of the quotidian. Race as a social and political identity for people belonging to Northeast is still a far cry. Race as a category for political action evince no state support in India. Unlike in the West where people are clearly distinguished on the basis of race (colour) with specific laws and institutions in place to deal with issues of racism, the same is absent in Indian cities. In India, 'caste' and 'tribe' are the legally recognized categories. And, the most marginalized among them, the 'Scheduled Castes' and 'Scheduled Tribes' are singled out for affirmative action. Not only is there a law in place, *The Scheduled Caste and Scheduled Tribes (Prevention of Atrocities) Act, 1989*, to deal with cases of discrimination and violence against them, the Constitution also spells out a number of measures that the state and its federal units must undertake for the uplift of the Scheduled Castes and the Scheduled Tribes in their respective jurisdiction. Not unexpectedly, this has not only reinforced the importance of tribe and ethnicity in the structuring of social relations, but also as bargaining tools for economic and political benefits.

Separate and Bounded: Ethnicity in the City

Closely related to what has been stated above, the people from Northeast have always led separate lives organized around tribe and ethnicity. The reason for this would be clear when we consider the social and political situation in the Northeastern states, which is sharply divided on lines of ethnicity, tribe, language, religion and topography. The divisions that structure the relations back home cannot simply be wished away when people from the different states and community move to the mainland cities. Though there have not been any report of clashes or conflicts among the Northeast communities in Delhi or any other city in India, a close observation of the everyday life of the Northeasterner in Delhi would make it clear that like most migrants, the Northeasterners too reproduce the structures and relations that characterize the society they leave behind. In other words, the social and cultural distinctiveness is carried along to the adopted home and reproduced in varied forms, beginning with the establishment of community and religious-based organizations and activities.

The social and economic environment in the city has not been able to dismantle the boundaries of ethnicity and tribes. This is not true of the Northeast alone but worldwide. Analysing the rise of ethnic politics amongst immigrants in New York City during the 1960s, Nathan Glazer and Daniel P. Moynihan debunked the 'melting pot' theory and asserted that melting does not happen when diverse groups of people migrate to the city for work and better livelihood.[10] Their study highlighted how the politics of ethnicity dominated the social and political scene of New York City during the period. A revisit to the site after a significant lapse of time affirmed their thesis; they found that the social equilibrium prevalent in the 1960s, which was driven between the alternatives of 'assimilation' and 'ethnic group status', began to take a different turn where the alternatives were 'ethnic group status' and 'separatism' (Glazer and Moynihan, 1973: xxiii). Their study shows it was ethnicity, and not occupation, that determined the status of individuals and groups in the city of New York (Glazer and Moynihan, 1973: xxiii). It has also been widely held that migrating to cities not only do not wipe away primordial identities, but also creates new sets of identities. Considering the political situation of ethnic communities from Northeast region, where there is not only conflict of political interest, but also excessive rhetoric of identity assertion, life in the city seems to have emerged as another arena where primordial identities can be strengthened and enhanced further.

The major ethnic groups from Northeast, such as Nagas, Mizos, Khasis, Kuki-Chin groups, Meiteis, Bodos and other groups, seem to have found their own niche in Delhi While to the local communities and other ethnic groups in the city they are popularly known by the generic term 'Northeast' or 'Northeasterner', internally each group has organized itself and constructed its own community life in various aspects while living in the city. Those ethnic groups that have adopted Christianity in large numbers have formed their own church like organisations and fellowships based on their ethnic nomenclature, such as, Khasi-Jaintia Christian Fellowship, Mizo Christian Fellowship, Naga Christian Fellowship, and other fellowships. Of course, being a place of worship any person supportive of the faith irrespective of ethnic or linguistic identity can attend or take part in devotional service and allied activities of any church or fellowship set up by a community. But the usage of ethnic nomenclature and linguistic medium in the conduct of the various rites and prayers meant that these organizations are basically intended for specific socio-cultural and linguistic groups. Some fellowships even debar non-ethnics from becoming members of the executive committee or holding of official positions. In such an exclusivist milieu, it is not surprising that denomination-based churches are hard to find while ethnic-based religious organizations and fellowships abound in plenty. Even in the rare case that denomination-specific church exists, it is also determined by tribal boundaries. Therefore, it is not religion *per se* that defines their identity. In fact, religion has not been able to serve as a unifying force that transcends the ethnic boundaries to create a pan-Northeast Indian identity.

For all the emphasis placed on Christian brotherhood, our data indicates Christianity has failed to create a pan-Northeast Christian identity. Rather, far from forging solidarity among the believers, as functionalists would have us believe, religion has become another site where distinction between groups is asserted and acted upon. Not only have churches been established on the basis of tribe and ethnicity, in some instances it has even got down to the level of sub-tribe, no matter how small their members might be in the city. Every Sunday, members of the group come from every part of the city and worship together in their respective tribal language, and amongst their own people. As devotional service and practices are often enacted in their own ethnic and tribal language, the mode of worship in the city is also likely to have been organized on that basis. While these re-enactments of ethnic and tribal identity may have to do with the modes and medium of worship that are traditionally followed by Christians in the Northeastern region, they act as obstacles to the establishment of pan-Northeast identity. This also perhaps explains why pan-Northeast Christian organizations and activities have not been quite successful in India, even though there are few of such.

The ethnic divide characteristic of religious bodies finds vivid reflection in the students' organizations and welfare bodies set up by the Northeasterners in Delhi. Every ethnic group has an apex student body, to look into the welfare and articulate the views and concerns of students belonging to the particular ethnic group. Besides the apex body, which represents the voice of the ethnic group as a whole, such as the All Naga Students' Union or All Assam Students' Union, there are also various tribe-based students' organizations which primarily cater to the needs and interests of their respective community members, for example, Tangkhul Students' Association, Bodo Students' Union, Khasi Students' Union and other organizations. Unlike other counterparts in cities in Western countries, where 'ethnic enclaves' not only shape their identity but also thrive on economic activity (Jan Lin, 2005 in Nancy Kleniewski (ed) 2005, 100–109), we are yet to see such phenomena in major scale, though some form of ethnic entrepreneurs from Northeast employing people from their own community is also taking place in Delhi (we will come back to this later). There are various modes and layers in which Northeast communities have organized their lives in Delhi. While this may have happened due to the rise in their population in the city, what is significant is that ethnic and tribal identities have been reaffirmed in the city where their presence is negligible in every aspect.

What emerges from the facts documented above is that there is significant variation in the construction of Northeasterners as the 'other' in metropolitan cities such as Delhi. While at one end, the Northeasterners are cornered and conceived as a community that is unified and singular; at the other end, we find that sharp differentiation exists at every turn of the social set up among the Northeast people. The identification of the Northeasterner as a racial category, therefore, is still in the process of finding recognition from within and without. In a highly generalized perception, physiological and regional criteria – race and culture – and in some instance religion have often been used as yardsticks to mark the people from Northeast as a community within the diverse social and cultural milieu of urban India. It is also yet to be ascertained what social, cultural or historical aspects can be utilized to define people from India's Northeast as distinct and different from people of other regions and cultural groups of the country. Be that as it may, what is significant is, though internal variation is a lived reality, in general, Northeasterners continue to be viewed as a monolithically 'strange' and 'exotic' group of people in the various social spaces and places of the global city they seek to make their home.

Notes

1. Pemberton, 1835. *The Eastern Frontier of Bengal.*
2. Alexander Mackenzie, The North-East Frontier of India, Reprinted 2001, Photographically reproduced from 1884

edition entitled, *History of the Relations of the Government with the Hill Tribes of the North-East Frontier of Bengal.*

3. Subir Bhaumik, 2010. *Troubled Periphery: Crisis in India's Northeast.* New Delhi: Sage Publications
4. For more on this, see T. Nongbri (2014), Chapter 1
5. 'Northeast migrants succeed at vocations – this makes them targets', *Times of India*, New Delhi, 5 March 2014.
6. Kamaladevi Chattopadhyay, 1978. *Tribalism in India,* Vikas Publication; Hamlet Bareh, 1970. *Gazetteer of Nagaland.* Kohima: Nagaland District Gazetteer's Unit.
7. 'BJP refers to northeast people in Delhi as immigrants', *The Hindu*, 3 February 2015. See also 'BJP corrects northeast "immigrants" mistake, Vision Document calls it clerical error', *First Post*, 16 February 2015.
8. Though the boundary between 'tribe' and 'ethnicity' is highly blurred, for instance, Horowitz defines 'ethnicity' as an umbrella concept that 'embraces groups differentiated by color, language, and religion; *it covers "tribes," "races," "nationalities," and castes*' (1985, 53, italics added), conceptually the two are distinct. In anthropological terms, 'tribe' refers to a set of people who are bound to each other by common descent, language or territory, whereas 'ethnicity' is a process that comes into existence when members of culturally distinct groups interact with each other. In other words, while tribe refers to the property of a group, ethnicity is an aspect of social relationship between groups, which may possess similar characteristics or goals, but see the other as culturally different from themselves (cf. Eriksen, 1993: 11–12). The pejorative connotation that inheres in the colonial construction of tribe, as a people who are 'primitive', 'superstitious' or at a lower level of social formation, has today led many communities earlier identified as tribes to abandon the concept and view themselves as 'ethnic groups'. This is particularly true of Africa where many countries in the continent have replaced 'tribe' with 'ethnic group(s)' to refer to its people. The case is somewhat different in India, though many tribes are increasingly resorting to the term ethnic group to distinguish themselves from the cultural other, the official recognition of the category 'tribe' as 'Scheduled Tribes' for purpose of

affirmative action meant that the term has not only come to stay, but also routinely invoked as a political tool by the designated and new claimants alike to assert their identity and/or to avail the benefits provided by the Constitution.

9. We will look into this matter in detail in a later chapter.
10. Nathan Glazer and Daniel P. Moynihan, 1973. *Beyond the Melting Pot: The Negroes, Puerto Ricans, Jews, Italians, and Irish of New York City*. Cambridge, MA: MIT Press.

CHAPTER 3

Social and Economic Profile of the Respondents

Contrary to popular perception, the social composition of Northeasterners who have moved outside their state is not homogenous in nature. This can be affirmed from the fact that not all persons who move out from Northeast are looking for work, or belong to a certain category such as landless labourers, or end up in large numbers in a few industrial units and factories. Nonetheless, the social and economic factors that are generally associated with migration, the 'pull' and 'push' factors seem to have determined most of their modes of outward flow in Northeast India too.

Movement of People from Northeast

Jan Breman notes that migrations among the landless workers in mainland India mainly took place due to the search for non-agricultural or non-agro-based work, and for better salary (Breman, 1996; Cf. Banerjee, 1983). The movement of people from the Northeast cannot simply be reduced to economic strategies directed to escape from agricultural works, as most of the persons who move out belong to the educated class, a sizable chunk of which comprised students, who leave the region in search of higher education, and civil services aspirants who come for coaching in the numerous teaching shops across the city in the hope of making it to the elite club of the Indian bureaucracy. As far as work-related migration from Northeast is concerned, the search for better job avenues and amenities seems to have played a significant role, as the higher perks in private sectors located in the metropolis attract many to the city.

However, not all Northeasterners located in Delhi can be defined as migrants in the ordinary sense of the term. Quite a sizable chunk comprised individuals employed in government sectors who move to the city as part of regular transfers in the profession. Many of these comprised personnel in the police force brought on time-bound deputation from different Northeastern states to look after the security of VIPs and VVIPs and other government establishments in the city. In more recent times, many have come as part of the contingent to man the newly created Special Police Unit for the North Eastern Region in the Delhi Police (more on this in Chapter 6). These along with officials in different central ministries and departments constitute a floating population of persons who come to the city for a fixed period of time and then return to their home cadre in the respective states after completing their tenure in the city. As stated at the outset, what makes up the largest segment of 'out-migrations' from India's Northeast are students who leave their home states and move to the cities for higher studies and search for a better future. These students constitute a new crop of youngsters, who have not only been educated in good schools, but also more adapted to the practices and different social and cultural environments characteristic of cities.

One situation that can be considered as a 'push' factor in the movement of Northeasterners is the volatile political situation in their home states. People in the Northeastern region have experienced armed insurrections from ethnic-based political organizations, which have resulted in violent skirmishes, and imposition of draconian laws such as the Armed Forces Special Powers Act (AFSPA), 1958, for many decades. Even now, some states in Northeast are still reeling under the imposition of AFSPA and other draconian laws, which makes living a normal life less secure. Some studies have also suggested that many people in Northeast have been affected by the trauma of conflict, which had taken place in the past.[1] Migration to other states and distant places has also been considered as consequences of trauma; escape from volatile situation is psychologically considered as a mode of coping with traumatic experiences.

Another factor that significantly contributes to the movement of people from Northeast India is 'relative deprivation' and underdevelopment of the region. The dearth of quality educational institutions and institutions of higher learning in key disciplines in most parts of the Northeast has pushed the youths into the cities (see in particular, Singh and Ahmad, 2012: 24–26). Further, the lack of infrastructure and good employment opportunities in their home districts and states have made the youth to look for other avenues in different places for better working conditions and livelihood. This has brought hundreds of youngsters from Northeast to take up jobs in the booming hospitality sectors and BPO workstations located in mainland Indian cities.

Social and Occupational Profile of Respondents

From the data we have collected through the survey, 93.02 per cent of the respondents have moved out from their native place and come directly to Delhi, indicating that they have chosen their destination with clear intention. The information also shows that most of the individuals have a rural background and originally inhabited in small towns, but highly exposed to Westernized culture due to their educational attainment as well as exposure to other cultures (see Table 1):

Table 1

Origin of Migration

Place of Origin	*Number*	*Percentage*
Home State	120	93.02
Other Places	0	0
'No Response'	9	6.97
Total	129	100

Some of the respondents mentioned that they have come from towns and cities, in some instances outside their own home states. Significantly, 46.51 per cent of the respondents stated that the family is their main point of contact in coming to Delhi, which suggests that many were not complete strangers to the place but already have family members or relatives living there before their arrival in the city. About 27.13 per cent of the respondents reported that they had taken substantial help from their friends and 13.17 per cent from their relatives while coming to Delhi, subscribing to what analysts call 'chain migration', where social relations and native ties play significant role in helping and motivating people from their own communities to move out of their 'homeland' for better prospects.

Table 2

Social Contacts of Migrants

Contact	*Number*	*Percentage*
Friends	35	27.13
Family	60	46.51
Relatives	17	13.17
Others	17	13.17
Total	129	100

Considering that most of the communities in Northeast were not traditionally accustomed to migrating to distant places for taking up new work or temporal settlement, the dynamics of chain migrations seem to have played a major role on the movement of Northeasterners from their home state(s). Of all the social ties that the respondents have relied on, the assistance of family members and friends are the most conspicuous among people moving to Delhi for the first time (see figures in Table 2). However, there are also instances where some individuals have utilized the services of 'others' in relocating to new places. From the data collected, more than 13 per cent of respondents relied on 'others' for help in settling down.

As far as occupation is concerned, the Northeasterners in Delhi have registered their presence in various sectors of the economy. The analysis of the occupational background reveals that 51.93 per cent of the respondents are students pursuing various courses in the universities and colleges in Delhi. Historically, students are the first category of people who have moved out from their native places and lived in distant places, where they are not only new to the cultural environment but also unfamiliar to the locals. The youth constitutes an educated class, which is more exposed to the outside world than the older generations; thus, more amenable to stay in different social situations. Our investigation reveals that many students choose not to return to their hometown on graduation, but take up professional jobs and get absorbed in the private sectors, or sit for the prestigious Union Public Services Commission (UPSC) examinations to join the coveted ranks of the Indian Administrative Service. While not everyone who aspired to, or have made the attempt, succeeded to make it to the elite service, many continue to live in the city forming a new class of the urban citizens.

Table 3

Occupational Profile of Migrants

Occupation	*Number*	*Percentage*
Government Job	28	21.70
M.N.C./Private Sector	19	14.72
Others	6	4.65
Student	67	51.93
'No Response'	9	6.97
Total	129	100

The high presence of students strongly suggests that most persons from Northeast who move to the city do so mainly in search of better education. This trend of student's flight from Northeast to other parts of India has come to signify one of the most common features of population movement in the Northeastern region. Satoshi Ota has observed that young students from Northeast have been motivated to study in the cities because of the ease of admission. In his opinion, they are able to get admission in good universities and colleges across the country with the help of the constitutional policy of 'affirmative action' (Ota, 2011: 53–74).

While it cannot be denied that India's reservation policy has definitely increased the access of the marginalized groups to education and government services, for reasons cited in the preceding chapter, it would be erroneous to view India's Northeastern region as coterminous with tribes. It would also be prudent to note that not all tribal students gain admission in educational institutions through the 'quota'. A perusal of the admission lists put up by universities in the city such as Jawaharlal Nehru University and University of Delhi reveal that tribal students are increasingly crossing the 'cut-off' points stipulated for the 'general category' in different disciplines. Besides, there are a number of students both from the reserved and unreserved categories who joined private institutes for various full- and short-term courses, such as business management, hotel management, hospital administration, information technology, food technology, computer science and other disciplines, where reservations simply do not exist. Reservations or not, all over India, including the Northeast, aspiring parents leave no stones unturned to secure admission for their wards in reputed colleges and universities, as this would ultimately help them gain access to better jobs and a secure future.

Among the employed, the highest number (21.70%) of respondents is in the government establishment followed by the private sector and multinational corporation (MNC, 14.70%), suggesting that people from Northeast find the city an attractive destination not only for short-term employment but also for building their career due to the vast opportunities it offers. What is noteworthy is the rising number of youngsters engaged in MNCs and private sectors, which is a recent trend of getting employment. Hospitality industry and BPOs have also absorbed numerous young people from Northeast as they are well polished and could speak English fluently. Some analysts have also observed that people from Northeast have brought certain work ethics in these sectors, as they possess the quality of integrity and sincerity in their work. Moreover, the distinctive Mongolian features have added a new dimension to the recruitment of people from Northeast, which lends a 'global image' to the firms that employ them particularly in tourism, health and hospitality industry. At the other end of the spectrum, the adaptability of different tonal modes in speaking English have made people from Northeast most sought after in the BPO sector.

On the wider plane, the presence of a large number of Northeasterners in the city has also given rise to a small number of Northeast self-employed entrepreneurs who cater to the needs of the community. In various localities in Delhi, numerous shops that cater to the specific needs of people from the region have sprung up. Food joints, clothes shops and small cigarette and *pan* stalls can be seen flourishing in localities where people from Northeast have substantial presence. Improvement in air connectivity between major Northeast towns and cities with the Indian mainland has facilitated the transfer of locally produced goods from the region into the cities. For instance, in Northeast populated Munirka one can get freshly plucked traditionally cherished fruits and vegetables directly air lifted from Imphal on a daily basis from shops run by Manipuri women. This has not only led to the emergence of a new breed of entrepreneurs who engaged in interstate trade and export, buying goods from local producers and transporting them to their compatriots in the city, but also served to reduce the distance between the local and the national economy, albeit at a very preliminary level.

Northeast Shops and Restaurants in South Delhi's Munirka

Image 1

Customers waiting delivery of their local favourites

Image 2

Tangkhul foods and vegetables just a call away

Image 3

Enticing flavours from Mizoram

Image 4

A menu suitable to your taste and pocket

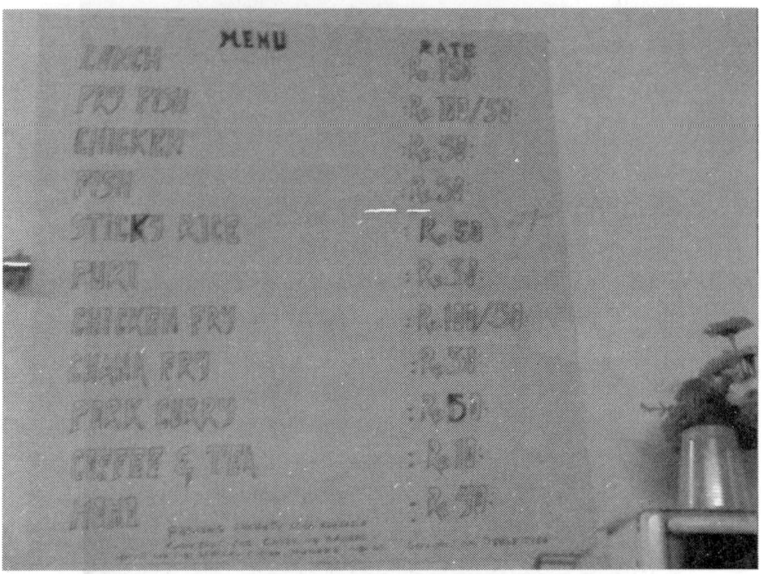

Image 5

Meiteilon in the heart of Munirka
(Note the list in puri printed on the wall)

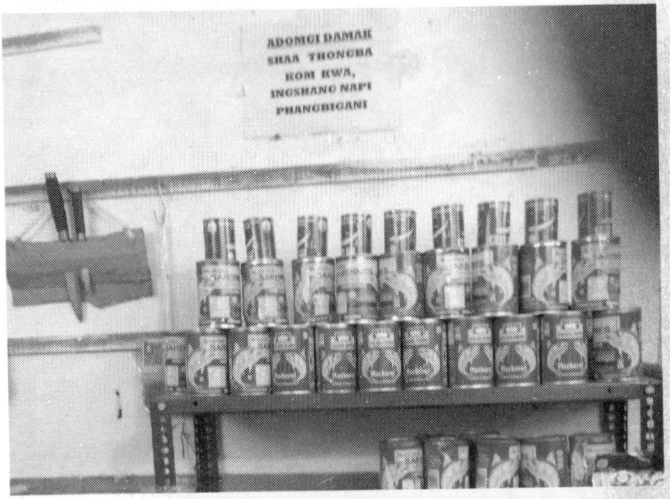

Image 6

Garden-fresh vegetables airlifted from Imphal

Image 7

A Naga restaurant in upmarket Green Park

Photographs: T. Nongbri

Apart from the economic aspect of employment generation and provision of livelihood to several migrant households, these ventures can be seen as modes of social and cultural adaptation that people from Northeast have adopted while putting up with unfamiliar city life. This measure forms one with other modes of social moorings, such as community-based students' organizations, welfare associations and Christian churches/fellowships that have been established by Northeasterners in Delhi.

Linguistic Background and Skills

Despite the fact that the cultural practices of Northeasterners are at sharp variance with their counterparts in Delhi, Northeasterners who have moved to Delhi display significant acculturation in terms of adapting to a new language (see Table 4).

Table 4

Languages Known

Language	*Number*	*Percentage*
Native language/Mother Tongue	120	93.02
Other NE Language	33	25.58
Hindi	103	79.84
English	114	88.37

Note: Figures in the table are not mutually exclusive as respondents speak more than one language. For reasons explained, though the percentage has been worked out from the total number of respondents they do not add up to 100.

Not as a rule, but through the medium of instructions in schools and by virtue of its status as the official language in the Northeastern states, most of the educated Northeasterners could speak fluent English. The same however is not true with Hindi. Though Hindi has been widely adopted as the preferred medium of communication along with English by the Central Government it is not commonly spoken in the Northeastern region as most states have their own state language and local dialects, which the people use for everyday communication with each other. However, as per our survey data, the Northeasterners in the city appear to have become multilingual in most respects. Apart from their respective native language, which continues to be the main medium of communication within the community, and English, which 88.37 per cent of the respondents are fluent, more than one-fourth (25.58%) can also speak other languages of the Northeast. The latter suggests that the cultural interaction among people from Northeast is also increasing. What really stands out is the widespread knowledge of Hindi, comprising a significant 79.84 per cent of our respondents, which can be considered as a classic form of 'acculturation' process. Given their historical unfamiliarity with the language, Hindi is a language that is learned in the later stages, or when the person moves into a new social milieu or place. However, language in urban spaces need not be seen as a marker of cultural identity, but a practical necessity for social interactions and compulsion imposed by the situation. Be that as it may, it needs to be noted that the desire to learn a new language reflects the Northeasterners' acceptance of the new social milieu within which they are located and constitutes part of a process of adaptation that leads to further exposure to other cultural elements in the host society.

With respect to gender composition, out of 129 questionnaires that we got back, four respondents did not specify their gender. Of those who did, the females at 49.61 per cent are slightly more than the males who stood at 47.28 per cent. The relatively higher presence of females indicates that Northeast women are taking equal part in earning and looking for jobs in whatever familial roles they occupy, be it wife, mother, sister or daughter. As most of the respondents in our survey comprised students, the high number of females also implies that there is equal focus and concern for women's education among the families and societies in Northeast India. However, this should not be seen as a phenomenon that is unique to the Northeast. Evidence reveals that this is a general trend in university education in the city that has been visible for quite some time.

Table 5

Distribution of Respondents by Gender

Gender	*Number*	*Percentage*
Male	61	47.28
Female	64	49.61
Gender not specified	4	3.10
Total	129	100

The varied feature in the social composition of the respondents reflects the changing modes of population movement to the city, and also the opening up of the region to external influences. The Northeastern region, which has often been described as landlocked and also hostile to outsiders is sending out not only its most valuable members, its sons and daughters, to other parts of the country in search of better avenues, but the number of migrants are also increasing year after year. And, it is not just to urban centres and some parts of the country that Northeasterners have migrated but they have also moved to the unlikeliest of places where people of their own kind can be seen. Interestingly, the increase in out-migration and presence of Northeasterners in other parts of the country has also reinforced the image of people from 'Northeast' as a singular entity that is distinct from other groups and cultures in the country. However, as our data shows, the process of actualization of such an identity remains to be seen among the Northeasterners themselves.

Finding Accommodation

For most of the newcomers to cities, the place where they live and work determine a lot about their experience of living in the city. Finding a house or room to stay can be considered as a first step towards the process of adapting to a new environment and 'place making'.[2] As McDuie-Ra has observed, the sense of place making by Northeasterners in Delhi has expanded and taken place in various sites, as indicated by the shops and churches run by Northeasterners that have sprung up across the localities in Delhi (2012b: 69–77). Apart from the landscape and social life, what is significant is the relationship that exists between the landlord and tenants: which includes the shared lifeworld as well as the cultural or social disjunctions. Northeasterners and their cultural life, being located in a geographical region that has less interaction with the people from other parts of India, have always evoked a sense of strangeness and intrigue in their encounter with the locals and landlords. The frequent media reports about the conflict and disjunctions between the Northeasterners and their landlord in Delhi suggest that their relationship is mainly based on economic considerations on both sides (income for the landlord and cheap accommodation for the Northeasterner), with little meeting point between the two in terms of culture, religion and other aspects of life.

Personal experiences that are commonly shared in the public domain also indicate that Northeasterners, whether new arrivals or old residents in Delhi, do find great difficulty in getting accommodation in posh colonies as well as nondescript localities in the city. Different racial features and lifestyle often aroused deep suspicion and reluctance in the landlords to let out their premises to the 'strange' looking Northeasterners. At the core of this discomfiture in the relationship between the landlords and tenants are the latter's food habits, which even the Delhi Police had taken special note of in their list of advice to Northeasterners residing in Delhi: not to prepare pungent foods such as bamboo shoots (*pashtenga, lung siej*) and fermented beans (*tung rymbai*) and fish items (*Ngari, tung tap*) that are relished by most people of Northeast and among some form part of their daily diet, but repulsive to most vegetarians and ritually conscious Hindus.[3] Most of the landlord's apprehensions are concerned with food, lifestyle, dress mode and cultural practices of the Northeasterners, which are very different from those of the general Indian population. Hence renting a home and sharing the same space with people with starkly different culture and lifestyles generates fear in the minds of many homeowners that this could hamper and disturb their own way of life. In certain cases, matters concerning morality[4] and choice of food items such as meat and fish have become the major stumbling blocks in getting accommodation for many Northeasterners, as these go against the religious beliefs and practices of the landlords.

Although casteism has not been strongly emphasized as a factor of discrimination against the Northeasterners, it cannot be discounted altogether. Recent studies on the residential pattern across the metro cities in India have also shown that caste structure, and not socio-economic status, plays significant role in determining the residence of individuals and groups (Vithayathil and Singh, 2012). The localities such as Munirka, Chiragh Delhi, Gandhi Vihar and Vikaspuri, where there are large concentrations of Northeasterners, also fall within the lower hierarchy in terms of the social status of the homeowners and amenities in the city. These are also the areas where the hold of caste and patriarchy are very strong, with the caste and village Panchayat serving as the supreme authority and custodian of the culture and tradition of the community. The propensity to choose certain localities and concentrate their population in those areas may have arisen due to diverse reasons. Whatever the reasons, evidence reveals the choices they make have serious implications on the security and pattern of relations between the Northeasterners and their immediate environment.

From the data collected through the survey (see Table 6), it is found that 68.99 per cent of respondents reside in rented accommodation. Considering the fact that half of them are students, the rest government employees and working professionals in private sector, and also for new arrivals in the city, rented accommodation may have turned out to be the only option available. At the same time, it is interesting to note the emerging trend of Northeasterners having self-owned accommodation in the city. Though the figure may be negligible in absolute terms, it is indicative of the growing affluence of Northeasterners and willingness to make the city a long-term place of abode, if not a permanent home.

Table 6

Types of Residence

Types	*Number*	*Percentage*
Rented Accommodation	89	68.99
Government Quarter	17	13.17
Self-Owned	5	3.87
Hostel	12	9.30
'No Response'	6	4.65
Total	129	100

With respect to students, only 9.30 per cent of the student respondents were able to get hostel accommodation, which clearly demonstrates that educational institutions in Delhi have not been able to take care of the needs of students coming from distant places. Given their financial status, few of the students could afford to take a room or stay as paying guests in better-off localities. The vast majority are forced to stay in the suburban villages located in various parts of Delhi where the rents are comparatively lower but inhabited by the more conservative and tradition-bound communities steeped in caste prejudice and patriarchy.

Out of 89 persons in our sample who had taken up rented accommodation to set up their home in the city, 43.82 per cent have relied on brokers to find their accommodation (see Table 7). This may have happened due to the mechanism that has been put in place in various localities in Delhi where renting is generally done through the service of local brokers, who usually charge 50 per cent of the rent each from the tenant and the house owners for availing their service. Renting through brokers has become an accepted *modus operandi* in various Delhi localities, which most of the migrants to the city have to go through as part of the initiation ceremony of life in the city. Further, the trend of taking a friend's help in renting still remains high. However, the mode of finding accommodation on one's own appears to be a rising feature. The mode of finding accommodation on one's own is indicative of the familiarity with the local populace and environment. Especially, for females such venture may be considered as rising confidence on their part, and yearning for independence, which has been accelerated by their earning capacities as well.

Table 7

Mode of Renting

Mode	*Number*	*Percentage*
Broker	39	43.82
Friends	23	25.84
Self	17	19.10
Other	10	11.23
Total	89	100

Relation with the Landlords and Locals

As stated before, the terms of relationship between the tenants and landlords may essentially be of an economic nature, but it also involves various terms of agreements and consensus while acquiring/giving the accommodation for renting. It is in the process of negotiation that many tenants and landlords not only agree to the terms, but also find out more about each other. Failure to agree on certain terms, or just by seeing the face of the person, the prospective tenants may be turned away.

Findings from the study presented in Table 8 reveal that a significant number (31.46%) of respondents reported that they faced problems in getting accommodation. Migrants from other parts of the country would have also faced problems in getting accommodation. The problems of Northeasterners, however, may have varied from other migrants due to the vast difference in culture and racial features with the local residents in Delhi and other metro cities.

Table 8

Problems in Getting Accommodation

Yes		*No*		*No Response*	
Number	*%*	*Number*	*%*	*Number*	*%*
28	31.46	37	41.57	24	26.96

While Northeasterners generally experience a hard time getting rented accommodation in the city, it has been affirmed that their relationships with the landlord do not always indicate much of negative responses. Majority of respondents (64.04%) stated that they have not received any complaint from their landlord(s) concerning breach of conditions agreed on (see figures in Table 9 and 10).

Table 9

Problems with Conditions Laid by Landlord

Yes		*No*		*No Response*	
Number	*%*	*Number*	*%*	*Number*	*%*
25	28.08	35	39.32	29	32.58

Table 10

Complaints for Breach of Conditions

Yes		*No*		*No Response*	
Number	*%*	*Number*	*%*	*Number*	*%*
4	4.9	57	64.04	28	31.46

The responses reveal that the most significant problem Northeasterners encountered is with respect to 'Security Deposit', which tenants are expected to shell out before signing the lease agreement with the landlord. The deposit, which is usually in the form of two to three months advanced rent that is refundable at the termination of the lease, is generally adopted to provide the landlord with a safety net in case a tenant defaults on the monthly payment of the rent. Our findings show that 59.5 per cent of the respondents found this problematic (see Table 11).

Table 11

Problems with Security Deposit

Yes		*No*		*No Response*	
Number	*%*	*Number*	*%*	*Number*	*%*
53	59.55	13	14.60	23	25.84

Notes: Percentages in Table 8–11 have been worked out of 89, the total number of respondents in rented accommodation.

Discussions on the issue carried out with cross sections of Northeasterners who lived in rented accommodation disclose that landlords rarely refund the full sum of the security deposited, but would arbitrarily deduct a significant portion of it in the name of recovering the cost of maintenance and repairs for breakages and other defacements, ostensibly inflicted by the tenants during their occupation of the property. Many Northeasterners interviewed expressed that they found this practice highly irksome. Some saw it as a surreptitious device used by landlords to extract more money from the hapless tenants.

Besides, what may appear to be cordial relations between landlord and tenants may actually carry various subtly hidden modes of discriminations. While most Northeast tenants have become quite familiar with the renting scenario in Delhi and are prepared to strike a more congenial relation with the host society, few find the conditions set down by the landlords reasonable. Many expressed the view that while conditions such as 'No Partying' and 'No loud music' are understandable, restrictions such as 'No guest in the room' and 'Do not cook or eat non-vegetarian food in the house or apartment' are clear infringements on the personal and cultural autonomy of tenants. By setting such standards, the tenants are not only given the space for accommodation, but gradually being compelled to follow the social practices of the landlord. The landlords setting the terms for tenants while giving accommodation to them, and even the tenants expect some strictures, is a widely accepted fact, but not of the kind that is patently inimical to their culture. Nonetheless, many people belonging to different culture and social practices or following different religion from which the landlord(s) practice usually find themselves gradually getting acculturated to the landlord's and the local value system. It is in this process of social adjustments and cultural adaptation that we tend to find instances of hostilities between Northeasterners and their landlords in cities across India.

Maintaining Old Cohesion and New Social Ties

When people move to a new place and social environment that is starkly different from their own locality, attempts are generally made to maintain or recreate the old structures and practices in the new settlement. These aspects come as ultimate response to the need for community and nostalgic desire to remain rooted in the tradition and life ways they left behind. Louis Wirth (1927) had used the term 'ghetto' to describe the social cohesions that people belonging to ethnic minorities maintain while living in a city. It denotes a social situation in which ethnic community live in isolation when confronted by different cultures. In the words of the author:

> It indicates the way in which cultural groups give expression when transplanted to a strange habitat: it evidences the constant sifting and resifting that goes on in a population, the factors that are operative in assigning locations to each section, and the forces through which the community maintains its integrity and continuity. (Wirth, 1927: 58, Cf. Wirth, 1938)

The mode in which cultural communities respond to strange social environment may vary in many ways, but the hidden undercurrent of maintaining cohesion remains a strong force that determines its social organizations and institutions. The case of Northeast communities living in Delhi represents an unusual situation of heterogeneous communities being clubbed together as one cultural group due to their shared socio-political history and association with a specific geographical region. Thus, their modes of responding to a new environment also vary from other communities that have moved to the city from their native places. In real terms, their sense of 'community' may turn out to be very miniscule in terms of association and institutions, and largely remain invisible to the dominant communities and local populations in the city. Their form of social cohesion has remained largely confined within the social unit of tribe and/or ethnicity, even if there is pan-tribal conglomeration at a larger level. In the city, we find that similar forms of societal associations are maintained where institutions based on shared tribal identity or belonging to the same tribe have become the central point of societal relationships. As such, the idea of Northeasterners constituting a single cultural group having close-knitted association may turn out to be a *perception from the outside, rather than the construction from within.*

The process of social mapping and place making of Delhi in terms of living in localities, worshipping, socializing and pattern of everyday practices is a factor that needs to be acknowledged while seeking to understand the social dynamics of Northeast communities in Delhi. However, these activities are extensively tied to the life within their community and its collectivity. Though such activities may also occur in relations with the people outside the community, the primary focus remains with the life of the community, which is again closely intertwined with the individual's life. For Northeasterners in Delhi, the relations that bind the individual with their community happen mostly around the public and cultural events, which take place regularly and annually. As a common annual festival, tribe-based students union in Delhi organizes 'Fresher's Party' and orientation programme every year at the beginning of the new academic session where all students belonging to the tribe would be provided a brief introduction on life in the city. On the religious front, again we find that tribe-based churches and fellowships play active role in organizing religious worship and celebrations throughout the year. Thus, even if Northeasterners have moved to a new place, their bonding with the community is never strained or cut-off in real sense, and by association. Not only the institutionalized practices, but also the parameters of associating with their own community and social and religious organizations remained more or less on the same line as in their home state. The relative difference that we may find is in the options that are offered to the migrants, and also emancipation that they get from living in the city as social constraints and pulls are much lesser. In certain circumstances, their busy work schedule and professions may hamper their active participation in community life. But by and large, members do make it a point to occasionally take part in them.

What is conspicuously lacking among the Northeasterners in Delhi is the presence of pan-Northeast social and cultural organizations based on the region as a whole, and even if such organizations came into existence they have not been active or given focal attention by the members. However, tribe and ethnic-based social organizations have been active in almost all spheres of community life in the city. Such institutions have served as the binding force for community life in the city and also as an extension of the way of life traditionally led in their ancestral village or native place.

Information gathered on community life in the city reveal that an overwhelmingly large number of respondents participate in community activity through attending worship services in church and other religion-based activities. The data shows that 74.41 per cent of the respondents regularly attend community-based church and/or fellowships while living in the city, whether they are working or studying (see Table 12). While at one level, this points to the deep religiosity of the Northeasterners, it is also possible that this practice may not be dictated by spiritual reasons alone, but as a means to keep in touch with fellow community members in a place where daily interaction is not possible by other ways. Attending religious gatherings is a regular feature in the towns and villages inhabited by Christians in Northeast India. Therefore, the practice of going to church on a regular basis could be one way of maintaining continuity of socio-religious practices and reproducing the life ways and mores of their homeland in the metropolis, thus recreating the social atmosphere which they miss in the city. In practical terms, attending worship services may also turn out to be the only time that persons belonging to a common faith and community get the opportunity to come together in a city that is populated by people of diverse beliefs and cultural practices. This could also be a survival strategy propelled by the sheer compulsion of living in a highly competitive and materialistic world where the only solace one can find is in religion and the company of one's co-believers.

Table 12

Modes of Maintaining Community Relations

Activities	*Number*	*Percentage*
Attending Church/Fellowship	96	74.41
Participation in Students' Union/Community Organization	40	31.00
Living in Locality Populated by Own Community	26	20.15
Others	20	15.50

Note: The answers are not mutually exclusive as respondents engage in multiple activities simultaneously.

Participation in faith-based activities is a vital factor that binds members of a community together, in the Durkheimian (Durkheim, 1915/1976)[5] sense. It would, however, be erroneous to view the Northeasterner as an insular community, uninterested in or impervious to influence from outside. What can be considered as the opening up of spaces for wider interaction takes place in the sphere of finding location for residence and relations established in educational institutions and places of work. While community organizations do play a valuable part in times of crisis, its role has not been seen so much in other spheres of community life and personal needs. The diversity in profession and financial stability of the individuals, as well as increasing exposure to people from other cultures and/or similar interests, may have made community-based organizations less important in their day-to-day life. Furthermore, individuals who are engaged in demanding professions or have full time jobs would hardly find time to actively engage in community works and festivities during working days. In like manner, choice of accommodation too depends to a large extent on an individual's paying capacity and convenience, for example, staying close to the work place or college. Due to all these factors, Northeasterners in Delhi may opt to stay in areas other than those inhabited by their own kind.

However, the level of choices for living in a locality indicates larger social dynamics at work in a multi-ethnic environment in the city. Numerous studies have emphasized that group choices for residential patterns is also indicative of social relations (Fong and Shibuya, 2005). Who one chooses to live with and share the neighbourhood has always been a matter of interest to sociologists engaging in urban studies. Processes of 'place making' and neighbourhood ties go together in shaping the social relations that are formed in the city, with one's own community and others. Therefore, while analysing the identity and dynamics of community life among the Northeasterners, we need to see whether the aspects of residence play a role.

In the following section, attempts are made to map the modes of interrelations between the Northeasterners and people from other community, as well as relationship with their own community in the city.

Attitude towards Intercommunity Relations

As far as modes of intercommunity interactions are concerned, Northeasterners have positive outlook towards cross-cultural relations. The responses gathered through the survey clearly suggest that there exist extensive interactions between the Northeast respondents and their counterparts from other communities in the city. To the query 'known persons outside the community', the responses are as high as 95.34 per cent (see Table 13). Though when it comes to level of being 'Comfortable in Interaction', the answer dropped down to 76.74 per cent, this is by no means an insignificant number (see data in Table 14).

Table 13

People Known Outside the Community

Response	*Number*	*Percentage*
Yes	123	95.34
No	0	0
No Response	6	4.65
Total	129	100

Table 14

Level of Comfort in Intercommunity Relations

Comfort Level	*Number*	*Percentage*
Comfortable	99	76.74
Not Comfortable	23	17.82
No Response	7	5.42
Total	129	100

Table 15

Interaction with Persons Outside One's Community

Category of Persons	*Number*	*Percentage*
People in College	76	58.91
People at work/office	55	42.63
People in Church	20	15.50

Note: Answers presented above are not mutually exclusive as respondents ticked more than one slot, which indicate that there is simultaneous interaction with persons from different classes and social background.

We also find that major interactions take place in colleges and offices, rather than in religious gatherings and ceremonies (see Table 15). By which it also means that on the secular plane, interactions across religious lines are much more, and Northeasterners do not stick to their own religious group in their daily lives. It is indicative of the extent of accommodation that people from Northeast have for integration with other communities. This may occur in the form of individual involvement with the activities of other communities and allowing people from other communities to take part in Northeast's community's affairs.

Northeasterners are still miniscule minorities in metro cities such as Delhi, and they are stranger to the cultural patterns of the local community. Instead of making people from Northeast turn to their own cocoon, the condition of being *stranger* may have actually helped them to venture out. In most instances the modes of interactions go beyond the formal relations that exist in offices and work places, and it is not only taken outside, but also moved into different aspects of life. The findings presented above also suggest that unlike the multi-ethnic cities in the West and other European cities, Delhi has much higher level of diffusion in residential patterns. Some factors such as temporal movement and inability to acquire residential areas and plots by migrants could have contributed to diffusion in residential patterns.

The reasons that the respondents have given for being comfortable or uncomfortable while interacting with people from other communities bring to the fore certain issues, which have generally been considered as barriers in cross-cultural interactions. Past experience and perception derived from one's own upbringing and cultural practices, all seem to have determined the level of comfort in cross-cultural interactions. However, interaction with the cultural other in everyday life is essential for building wider relations, which could break down the old stereotypes and also form better understanding of other cultures.

Factors Promoting Intercommunity Relations

While most of the respondents have indicated positive attitude towards intercommunity relations, the reasons given for being comfortable in the company of people from other community depends much on the perception about the other person's attitudes or behaviour and their 'understanding of cultural differences'. Some respondents have simply stated that their comfort in relationship with people from other community is based on *'same perspectives towards life'*, *'similar attitudes'*, *'polite in nature'* and so on. We may not be able to perceive how deep the level of interactions are in these circumstances, but close examination of the answers indicate that this attitude usually occurs with respect to co-workers and colleagues who in turn became friends, where the forms of interactions are part of their professional or student life. In certain instances, the level of interactions also moves to the next stage of intimacy and involvement with each other's personal life, where conflicts and differences are prone to take place. Analysis reveals, the so-called similarities between the interacting individuals are mostly based on the parties' personal traits, rather than that of their respective community's social practices and religious beliefs. Some respondents have even expressed the reason for their being comfortable as: *'They let me do my work. As long as they don't interfere in my business, I am comfortable with them'*. Such stances are clear indication of marking boundaries and level of interactions, and also highlight a mode of social relationship that is heavily dependent on mutual regard and respect. Further, such attitude also denotes that some Northeasterners have marked personal spaces where they are not willing to allow others to intrude, whether it is at the workplace or in their private lives.

The level of comfort that Northeasterners experience in their interaction with people from other community reflects the value placed on reciprocity, where helping hands are being extended and taken from either side of the group. What comes across from the respondents' responses is appreciation for the help being offered and given by their counterparts. On the query of reasons for being comfortable in having interaction with people outside their community, respondents have succinctly expressed: *'They give me support when I needed it and told me to call/contact them any time in case of trouble'*; *'Yes, by interacting and helping each other in times of need; 'Yes, sharing ups and downs, and helping each other when need arises'.* This freewheeling help being extended and offered in times of need seems to have served as a cementing force that transcends the barrier of language, religion and geography, whereby cultural and regional differences are set aside, but see the 'other' simply as a human being with common strengths and frailties. Reaching out to others in times of need and simple acts such as working together or sharing of 'class notes' in the context of students have been described as the foundation for healthy interactions by Northeasterners.

Another significant factor that has contributed to cordial relationships between Northeasterners and their counterparts are acceptance of 'who they are' and their cultural practices. Some sections of respondents have been quite appreciative that cultural difference has not come in the way in their modes of interaction, and their close acquaintances are able to understand and accept the Northeasterners' distinct life ways and work. Some respondents wrote: '*good friends are hard to come by, fortunately I have some who are trustworthy, broadminded, understanding, and accept me as I am*'. Another respondent expressed that: '*apart from getting along, their acceptance of my difference make it all the more easier* (sic)'. These responses can also be considered from certain aspects as acceptance of the concerned individual's personality type and behaviour. However, the larger context in which such social and personal acceptance of the individual is taking place also indicates situations where cross-cultural interactions have worked out in positive terms.

We can assume that acceptance of the cultural difference and life ways of the Northeasterners by their fellow students and colleagues at the personal level are good starting points towards building a more conducive cross-cultural coexistence in the city. However, it is a common social practice that the treatment and attitudes towards known persons and strangers significantly vary in different contexts and circumstances. And, the overwhelming positive attitudes shown by our respondents on having interaction with people from outside their community also highlighted a significant feature that they have shelved their 'exclusive' attitude to the backstage when it comes to interactions at the personal level.

The account narrated above takes on sharper significance when we put it alongside information gathered through interviews and conversations with some Northeasterners who lived as tenants in the city. To begin with, it is important to recognize that social interaction is never a one-sided affair but involves mutual understanding and concern for each other by the parties involved. Narratives of experience gathered through conversations with informants and acquaintances illustrate this fact.

In one instance, Angela from Meghalaya narrated that she shared a cordial relationship with her landlord and landlady in North Delhi in whose house she lived before shifting in with a friend in South Delhi. The landlord, an official in a nationalized bank, was posted outside the city leaving his wife and young daughters in Delhi. Hence Angela's presence was a blessing in disguise for the landlady. Besides providing companionship to each other, the two women forged a close working relationship, with Angela bringing gifts for the girls when she returns from vacations and coached them in their homework whenever they had problems with their study. In turn, the landlady allowed Angela to watch television in her drawing room and use her telephone to receive calls from her family (those were the days when mobile phone was a luxury for students). But the landlady also had her conditions, which Angela was bound to obey: she should not prepare or bring non-vegetarian food into the house, should not have parties or social gathering, or allow her visitors to smoke because she has a *mandir* (prayer room) in a room next to the leased out apartment. To sustain the relationship without inviting any tension, it was imperative that Angela adhered to these conditions. Though she sometimes felt the pinch that she could not exercise the freedom to invite her friends over to 'loosen up' and share a meal of pork and beef, in the interest of amicable relations she put up with it.

Another narrative illustrates the bond that characterizes the relations between a middle-class landlord and the Northeast tenants. The narrative concerns Dino and his sister who have come to Delhi for entrance examination coaching and a course in Delhi University respectively. Failing to get a hostel, they took up a rented accommodation in the house of an upper-caste Punjabi family, the landlord was an engineer with the Haryana Government and his father a transporter with permits to operate interstate buses in three North-eastern states. This business connection has made the family quite familiar with the region and its people. With this familiarity, and the fact that the brother-sister duo are a quiet and modest sort, no conditions were imposed on their timings, friends or food, except that they should pay the monthly rent in cash by the fifth of each month. Initially the relationship between the landlords and the tenants was restricted to the exchange of courtesies. Gradually the interaction grew. When the bus permit to one of the states expired, the grandfather asked Dino whether he knew the Commissioner of Transport whom he was meeting for renewal of the permit, to which Dino replied in the negative. But what brought the tenants closer to the family was the alcoholic problem of landlord's son. The landlord's son, who works with his grandfather in the transport business and is otherwise a sober and gentle type, is an alcoholic prone to excessive violence whenever he imbibes alcohol. Initially, the brother and sister discretely kept away thinking it best not to intrude into the private crisis of a family. But when the frequency and pitch of violence reached a stage where non-action could endanger the lives of the family, Dino was forced to intervene, an act that considerably sobered down the drunken son. In subsequent episodes of violence the landlady, whom Dino and his sister addressed as 'aunty', would send for Dino to pacify and calm down her son. Surprisingly, the son who would not listen to anyone and even became more violent when approached by his parents and kin would sober down to Dino.

A year later, Dino cleared his entrance test for a postgraduate course in Chandigarh and his sister got into a hostel in Delhi University. When they gave notice to leave the house, the landlady had tears in her eyes.

In another case, Parte a student from Manipur was all praise for her landlord's family, who she states are very caring. When she received a call from home to say that her mother had been hospitalized with a serious illness, they not only helped her book her tickets but also dropped her to the airport.

Yet another example comes from a pastor-in-charge of one of the Northeast Christian Fellowships in the city. The pastor who lives in a popular South Delhi locality reports a harmonious relationship with his landlord. Contrary to the experience of many, the landlord not only imposed no restrictions on their frequent visitors and devotional service held in the house, but also exchanged sweets and cakes on each other's religious festivals. He narrates an interesting incident, which brings out the degree of trust and regard that underlines the relations between the landlord and the tenant. Once his wife had prepared a dish of the 'infamous' fermented beans. To prevent the odour from hurting the sensibilities of the other residents in the building, she had kept all the doors and windows in the apartment shut, but still could not stop the smell from escaping. Unbeknown to them, the landlord's son was up on the terrace with his baby daughter. Struck by the pungent smell as he passed the pastor's door on his way down the stairs, he stopped and looked at the child in his arms. Thinking his little baby had soiled her diaper he opened her wrap and peered at it. Finding nothing amiss, he restored her wrap and quietly proceeded down the stairs without as much as a glance at the tenant's door.

The cases narrated bring into sharp relief the complexity and heterogeneity of the experience of the Northeasterners in Delhi. While some are at pains to adjust to the irrational demands of landlords, others are able to strike a harmonious relationship building trust and coming to each other's aid in times of crisis, which points to the commonality of human problems and sentiments that transcend cultural and geographical boundaries. At the same time, it cannot be denied that physical proximity between culturally divergent groups is prone to spark conflict due to stereotypical conceptions from either side of the cultural divide, where a person is socialized and brought up. It would be prudent to take a close look at these points of contention, if we are to have a realistic understanding of the problem.

Points of Contention in Intercommunity Relations

It is important to take note of the fact that 17.82 per cent of the respondents have mentioned that they are not comfortable in having interaction with people outside their community. This relatively modest figure apparently highlights that most Northeasterners have not faced much problems in having interactions and also have positive attitude towards cross-cultural relations. However, we cannot simply ignore the problem in cross-community interactions and relations, which take place at various levels. On quantitative terms, these problems may seem miniscule, but left unattended they have the potential to create social disharmony in the locality where numerous communities live and work side by side.

The reasons given by the respondents for being 'uncomfortable' in dealing with people from outside their community indicate that their problems in interaction occurred mainly due to differences in cultural practices and personal attitude. The inability to accept each other's cultural practices and preference for basic things such as food and dress also seem to have hampered modes of interaction for those who have problems in cross-cultural interactions. However, in numerous instances personal prejudice and stereotypical understanding of the other person or group's social life has also determined the hostility and apprehensions of one another.

Some respondents have simply stated that *it's hard to trust them* and they are *reserved in nature*, which is a blanket assumption of 'mainlanders' as not being trustworthy or are unfriendly and unaccommodating by nature. It also indicates that Northeasterners do have stereotypical conceptions of 'mainlanders' and such ideas have determined their perspective and responses towards them. Investigation indicates it is a case of prejudice that is shaped more by social circumstances and personal experience than by societal upbringing and cultural context. In the majority of cases, Northeasterners have not had very happy relations with the mainland people who migrated into the region for business and service, such as petty businessmen, soldiers and government officials who manned the various organs of the state machinery, hence their prejudices have been shaped largely by past experience of the community and not on abstract conception of 'self' and 'other'. Discussion on the issue with cross sections of persons from different states of the region revealed mixed experiences. While some reported of long-term friendships formed in schools and colleges, who in the course of studying and working together have come to develop mutual trust and regard for each other, there are also others whose impression of the mainland population is not so positive.

The analysis of answers on social interaction indicates similar veins of frictions in cross-cultural interactions, which occur by way of extending the prejudices. Those respondents who mentioned that they feel uncomfortable in interactions have stated that: *they are mean, they look down upon us*; *they have prejudice against us* and *some of them are hell bent on making you uncomfortable*. Further, the respondents also mentioned that the frictions in interactions occur, as the dominant communities are *being conservative regarding nature of our society's norms*. The perception that the local communities tend to misunderstand and unfairly judge their culture and life ways proved to be a major barrier to having cordial relationships. Here, we noticed that the problems in interactions shifted towards the issue of misunderstanding and intolerance in everyday encounters. These experiences may also shape the long-term relationships that individuals living in the city share. Moreover, the preconceived notions about each other seems to have only been reenforced when interactions go haywire or turn out to be filled by hostile attitudes.

On the level of actual difficulties that people from Northeast find hard to overcome pertains to religious and cultural practices. The Northeasterners see the difference in food habits, religious practices, aesthetic sense and lifestyle as major factors that act as obstacles to healthy interactions between them and their counterparts from other community. The real barriers in intercommunity relations, as per the respondents' statements, came from strongly held cultural practices and attachments such as religion and food habits. These differences may seem inconsequential and easily reconcilable by partial accommodation from either side of the cultural divide in cosmopolitan areas, but certain practices remain constant for individuals and groups even when they move to a new location in search of job and educations.

Evidence from the field suggests it is not unreasonable to believe that changes might have taken place among the Northeasterners who have moved to the city, while adapting to the living conditions in the new settlement. But with respect to their beliefs and practices, the data reveal the Northeasterners have not altered very much. As per the findings of this study, a high proportion of respondents are active participants in church-related activities and devotional services, which indicate that religious belief and practices have remained a constant feature in the life of Northeasterners in the Indian metros. Lending complexity to the matter is the fact that most of the religious practices of the Northeasterners do not sync well with the beliefs and practices of the local community in the city. Quite a sizable segment of the Northeast population follows Christianity, which sharply varies from the religious belief and practices adopted by the local community, where Hinduism is the dominant religion followed by Islam. Of course, clash and conflicts in the form of communal violence centring on religion witnessed in other parts of the country, such as those in Orissa (see in particular Kanungo, 2008, 2012) or the Hindu-Muslim violence in Gujarat (Varadarajan, 2002), have not come to the fore in the context of the Northeasterners. However, increasing vandalism of churches in the city and other northern Indian states has created a feeling of unease and insecurity among the religious minorities, which has acted as obstacles to intercommunity relationships. The religious differences have invariably contributed to the distance between Northeasterners and the local community, which does happen in terms of not only beliefs but also ritualistic practices. Most of the Christian Northeasterners are unlikely to take part in the rituals and festivals of the local community, starting with the landlord and neighbours, and it leads to divergence in perspective towards life. Further, with this ritualistic distance, the sense of community building with the locals is unlikely to grow. As Duncan McDuie-Ra notes, we may find that people from Northeast have greater attachment to the place, rather than the community and people living in their neighbourhood (2012b op cit.). This may have emerged due to variety of factors, nonetheless the divergence in sense of community building and belongingness may have played a vital role in it.

One aspect that Northeasterners have been noted for is their exotic food habits. Though local variation in food preparation exists among the Northeasterners, in general their taste and types of food consumed are at sharp variance with the diet of the dominant community. Apart from beef, one food item that has been at the centre of attention is fermented bamboo shoots and fish, which give out a highly pungent aroma that is appetizing for most Northeasterners but unbearable for the uninitiated. Most of the Northeasterners consume this food item on a regular basis, and this food item continues to be an integral part of their diet even after they have migrated to the cities.

Food *per se* may have little to do with a people's larger identity, but consumption of certain food considered ritually impure by the dominant population have become major points of contention between Northeast tenants and their landlords and/or neighbours, so much so that today it has ended as their identity marker as prospective landlords began to ask what food they consume whenever people from Northeast go for house hunting. Though people from other cultural and social background may also consume similar types of food, they may not be doing it openly as it goes against the dominant ethos of their belief systems. However, there are no sanctions against beef and pork in the religious belief and values of the Northeasterners either in the traditional belief system or in Christianity, though some clans observed a taboo towards certain plants and animals that are regarded as their totem.

Legal opinion in India considers 'right to food' as a fundamental right that is integral to 'right to life' enshrined in Article 21 of the Constitution (see in particular Sheela Barse, 1996: 69–80). However, the right to determine 'what to eat' has become a matter of serious contention with the rise of Hindu fundamentalism, which views the consumption of food that are banned to Hindus by the religious minorities as an affront to the nation, notwithstanding the fact that India is a signatory to the UN Covenant on Economic, Social and Cultural Rights, 1966 that seeks to protect and uphold the cultural practices (this include diet) and traditions of its citizens. While the Indian Constitution proclaims that India is a secular state firmly committed to the principles of equality, liberty, justice and fraternity, objections raised to the culinary preference of the minorities by the dominant communities not only poses serious challenge to the country's secular credentials, but also act as a major obstacle to cross-cultural interactions.

Our data reveals that, in general, people from Northeast do not have problems in having relationships with the local population and people from other community. In fact, except for a small minority who expressed some sense of discomfort, the large majority of respondents seem to have strong inclinations towards extensive intercommunity interactions. However, they are also strongly wedded to their religious beliefs and practices and the *much censured* dietary habits. It remains to be seen to what extent the Northeasterners will be able to hold on to their much debated diet amidst the persistent call for vegetarianism in the name of health and nonviolence on the one hand, and the coercive diktats of landlords, on the other hand. The recent incident in which the Union Minister of State for Home, who hails from Arunachal Pradesh, was forced to publicly retract his statement that he and his family consumed beef, as an expression of solidarity with his Party's support to the Rashtriya Swayamsevak Sangh's (RSS) call for nation-wide ban on cow slaughter,[6] makes the question highly significant for the Northeasterners.

Notes

1. Sanjoy Hazarika, 2011. *A Measure of Impunity – The Impact of Conflict on Women in Nagaland and Assam*, Centre for North East Studies, Jamia Millia Islamia.
2. Duncan Mcduie-Ra, 2012. 'The "North East" Map of Delhi', *Economic and Political Weekly,* Vol. XLVII, No. 30, pp. 69–77.
3. 'Security Tips for Northeast Students/Visitors to Delhi', Booklet issued by Delhi Police, Delhi, 2007. The booklet includes advice to Northeast girls not to wear 'revealing' clothes and suggestions about cooking 'smelly' food without creating a ruckus with neighbours. The tips raised the ire of Northeast students who view the advice as insensitive (see also, 'Delhi "Profiles" to Protect – Police Booklet for Northeast Students Betrays Prejudice', *The Telegraph*, 10 July 2007).
4. Due to their way of highly Westernized dressings and free intergender interactions, locals have often construed Northeasterners as generally loose in moral characters. However, this conception has much to do with the cultural disconnect, rather than the actual practices prevalent in their community life.

5. Durkheim, Emile, 1915/1976. *The Elementary Forms of Religious Life.* London: George Allen & Unwin Ltd.
6. 'Can Anyone Dare Me from Eating Beef? Kiren Rijiju Dares Mukhtar Abbas Naqvi', *First Post,* 27 May 2015. Accessed on 9 February 2016; also 'After Controversy over Remarks, Minister Kiren Rijiju says I Was Misquoted,' NDTV News footage, 27 May 2015.

CHAPTER 4

Racism and Social Discrimination

Issues and Contestation

In recent times incidents of discrimination and atrocities against Northeasterners in the major cities of India have made headlines in the national dailies, bringing the issue of racial discrimination against people of Northeast in metropolitan cities across India into public debate. India has generally been recognized as the land of diversity in various terms; however, the question why Northeasterners have been marked out as a distinct group and targeted in many parts of the country has often been pondered upon time and again.

Situating the Problem

As a sizable segment of the people of Northeast belongs to a different racial stock from the rest of the country, race has often been viewed as one of the main factors for the discrimination (McDuie-Ra, 2012b: 69–77; Thounajam, 2012). Recent studies that have been carried out to analyse the problems of Northeasterners in cities across India have also considered racism as one of the main reasons. In a survey carried out in 2011 by a Delhi-based NGO North East Support Centre & Helpline on the atrocities against Northeasterners in Delhi, it was found that 86 per cent of the people face racial discrimination (NESCH, 2011). The study also brings to light another startling fact that law enforcing agencies were not willing to extend their help to people from Northeast when they go to file cases in the police station. A study carried out by the V.V. Giri National Labour Institute also discloses that numerous people from Northeast have faced verbal abuse and name-calling in the localities where they live (Ramesh, 2012).

All these studies may have affirmed the perception that atrocities against the Northeasterners are racial in its forms and intent. However, by what standard this conclusion has been reached can be questioned from various perspectives. We may also need to question whether all forms of discrimination towards the Northeasterners can be wholly considered as racial discrimination. Some of the discriminations may pertain to cultural practices and religious beliefs, and also in some cases it may be the outcome of casteism, which is quite rampant in mainland India. However, race as a factor for social discrimination cannot be discounted altogether as large groups of people from Northeast do belong to a distinct racial category, which is at sharp variance with the local population. This is not to say that people of Mongolian racial stock are confined to Northeast. Large segments of the population in the Himalayan belt stretching from the Ladakh region in Jammu and Kashmir, Jaunsar-Bawar in Himachal Pradesh, Garhwal and Kumaon in Uttarakhand to Darjeeling in North Bengal share racial similarities with people from Northeast. But in the eyes of the Indian 'mainstream', the Mongoloid feature is primarily associated with the Northeasterners as their presence in the city began to reach exponential proportion.

Further, what has been passed off as racial discrimination may also entail some kind of xenophobia as doubts have frequently been cast on the political identity of the people from the Northeastern region. Often the people from Northeast have been considered as originating from Nepal by the locals in Delhi (Ramesh, 2012): a view which people from

Northeast have strongly resented as they are not only of different nationality but also belong to vastly different social and cultural universe to those identified with. Northeasterners have also been frequently taken for Tibetans especially by the Delhi Police, a regular occurrence which has put the Northeast youth through umpteenth harassments particularly in the wake of India's attempt to woo China, which had strong reservations to the Indian Government's stand on Tibet and its friendship with its spiritual head, the Dalai Lama. That there could also be a caste angle to the discrimination cannot be completely ruled out. People from Northeast follow diverse faiths and fall under various social categories, but in the attempt to impose homogeneity on them, they have been perceived by the local people as belonging to the generic category 'tribal' society. As a concept, 'tribe' is a colonial construct that carries a derogatory or pejorative connotation of 'uncivilized', 'barbaric' or 'primitive' people. In terms of social practices, the tribes in India especially those in the Northeast lie outside the hierarchical order of caste, but because of their dietary habit, which as noted in the preceding chapter, include beef, pork and fish in their daily diet, they have often been construed as lower than the Dalits. The strong presence of Christianity among the Northeasterners is also another factor that has pushed them away from the social order established by Hinduism, India's dominant religion. Thus, seen from the perspectives of caste hierarchy, Northeasterners occupy a social position that is vulnerable to all forms of social atrocities. While the attacks on Northeasterners may have stemmed from their marginal position in the Hindu social order, being the perennial 'outsider' make them soft targets for social deviants and prejudicial persons in the locality where they live and work. Existing evidence reveals that the outcomes of these prejudices have been quite appalling, as many Northeasterners have faced sexual harassment, molestations, and loss of life in the city. Many of the acts of discrimination began with innocuous remarks such as teasing and joking. But the matter seldom stops there. Going by media reports and the police records, many Northeasterners have ended up as victims of rape and physical assaults, thereby posing serious threat to the life of hundreds of persons who come to the city in search of better education and employment opportunities.

Mapping Discrimination

In the present study, attempts have been made to identify the forms of discriminations and the perpetrators of atrocities towards the Northeasterners. While available studies on atrocities towards Northeasterners have taken note of the extent and degree of racial assaults, they have not given much focus on the attackers and where the acts are directed. In our study we have tried to identify the instances of discriminations and the relation of the object of discrimination to the persons who indulge in such actions, whether they come from 'known persons' or 'strangers' to the victim. Further, we also have tried to analyse the mechanisms that people from Northeast employ when they encounter atrocities. To understand the actual discriminations experienced by Northeasterners in the city, special questions have been framed to map the reactions of people to the Northeast folks' dressing style and physical appearance. While the sartorial is concerned with aesthetic sense and cultural orientations, physical feature of the person has to do with his or her racial background. The reactions to both the aspects may not always be the same, as dress has much to do with class and fashion and physical body is a naturally given feature. We may say that perceptions towards Northeasterners by the local community and other cultural groups in the city have been largely shaped by their own social and cultural contexts.

The reactions to dressing styles as reported by our respondents indicate that they have been marked out by their sartorial taste as well. The analysis of the responses presented in Table 16 reveal that more than 65 per cent persons in our sample have encountered some form of comments about the way they dress, while 34.1 per cent did not face any of such. As people who have come from a geographical region, which has been seen as Westernized in their religious belief and way of life, it made them stand out in the midst of different cultural practices.

It is ironical that Northeasterners, who are supposed to come from remote areas and peripheral region, have to face flak for wearing Westernized clothes in the city. In most cases, young people from Northeast have discarded their traditional wear in favour of Western-styled clothing for a long time and use the traditional dress only on special occasions. Therefore, the reaction to dress does not seem to have come from the exoticism that is often associated with traditional attires of tribes and other distant communities. But, it may have come from the dressing sensibilities of the local community and their social context, where there are more adherences to traditional attires. On the part of the Northeasterners, their earnings through employment may have helped them in enhancing their purchasing power, which in turn has enabled them to dress up in accordance with their favourite taste and style. The nature of lifestyles in the city with its share of personal freedom and autonomy could also have influenced their dressing sense to a new level where it is generally assumed that the people would be characterized by more openness in sensibilities and thinking.

Table 16

Reactions to Dressing Style

Frequency	*Number*	*Percentage*
Occasionally	59	45.73
Most of the Time	26	20.15
Not at All	44	34.10
Total	129	100

We also find that more than 45 per cent of our respondents face occasional comments about their dressing, which is not a small figure in any sense of the term. It highlights the fact that such reactions could have come from persons belonging to varied caste or class. Further, 20.15 per cent reported to have faced such negative reactions to their dressing style most of the time, by which it would also mean their dressing sensibilities have been considered as 'outrageous' from certain viewpoint.

Dressing does not only mean clothes alone, but also include hairdos, makeup and ornamentation, which makes the experience of negative reactions to dressing not women's issue alone. While women have been the usual targets of negative comments over their clothes and makeup, Northeast men too have received a fair share of snide remarks over their different hairstyles and tattoos, a fact that finds strong affirmation in the brutal experience of Nido Tania and his subsequent death in the hands of Delhi shopkeepers who fatally beat him up when he reacted to their poking fun of his hairstyle.

In contemporary times, dressing styles of the youngsters have drawn flak from the elders and cultural groups in many parts of the country. While the younger generation seems to be moving ahead with the fashion of the day, we find that the elders and followers of traditional practices have opposed the changes as they are deemed to go against the ethos of the past. Some organizations have gone to the extent of attacking youngsters in public places who are seen to have dressed inappropriately.

In contrast to the dressing sensibilities generally seen in other parts of India, we need to take note of the fact that societies in Northeast have shown more tolerance towards dressing patterns of the youths. While mild admonishments may come from elders that the youth should dress more appropriately, public criticisms of their dress sense are rarely heard. This sharply contrasts with their experience in the city where adverse comments on their dressing style and looks are a regular feature. There have been various instances in the metros cities where women have been at the centre of attack for the way they dress, with the police giving their own directives about dressing and assumptions about the lifestyles of youngsters. Thus, Northeastern youths may not be the only target for 'inappropriate' dressing, but dressing in different ways and their exotic looks that stand out from the local population seems to have added steam to the stereotypical conception of their way of life.

To capture the actual acts of racial discrimination, we need to understand the manner in which people from Northeast experienced their everyday life in the city. To find the exact extent and reaction of the people from other culture and race, when they encounter Northeasterner we asked the persons in our sample to list the number of times they experienced negative reactions in their social interactions and who the perpetrators are, strangers or acquaintances.

From the responses catalogued in Table 17 we find that numerous respondents affirmed that they have faced some form of harassment due to their physical features. If we add up all the categories that have faced racial discrimination, the percentage of persons that have faced harassments comes to over 79 per cent, which indicates that the actual situation of racism in the city is quite pervasive, whereas only about one-fifth (20.93%) of respondents reported that they have not faced any form of harassments on account of their physical feature. We also find that the occasional harassments to the respondents are also quite high. Though such atrocities may have occurred in unsuspecting moments and places, it shows that people from Northeast face some form of mistreating in their everyday life.

Table 17

Reactions to Physical Features

Frequency and By Whom	*Number*	*Percentage*
Occasionally	43	33.33
Not At All	27	20.93
By Strangers	48	37.20
By Friends	11	8.52
Total	129	100

The harassment by strangers, as per the respondents' indication, is another aspect that has happened rampantly. From the data collected, it is quite clear that people from Northeast have been soft targets of acts of harassment when they go out to work or move about in the locality. As many of the cases may seem innocuous mischief and petty pranks by unruly elements, they are unlikely to make an issue of these experiences. But what makes the matter highly significant is the fact that the same unruly elements do not behave in the same way with the locals, many of who turned a blind eye when the acts were perpetrated on the Northeasterners. It would be prudent to note that it is such show of indifference than the unruly acts themselves that have served to create a feeling of alienation among the Northeasterners and widened the emotional gap with the local community. Some respondents have also reported that it is not just strangers alone who made adverse comments on their looks, but their friends as well occasionally use racial slurs at their physical features.

The forms of discrimination that people from Northeast face in Delhi do not end with simple acts of harassments and teasing. It has been frequently highlighted by the mass media that there have been numerous cases of rape and murder of Northeasterners in Delhi. Of course, we need to take note that people from Northeast are not the only group of people who have become victims of crime and criminal activities in the city. Nonetheless, in order to gauge the magnitude of the crime that has been perpetuated to people from Northeast, we have attempted to know the instances of actual cases of crimes being committed to Northeasterners in Delhi. In a previous study conducted by North East Support Centre and Helpline, the report shows that there have been 96 cases of crimes being committed on Northeasterners in Delhi between the years 2005 and 2011 (NESCH, 2011: 24).[1] The nature of crime covers a wide spectrum of acts, ranging from rape, murder, human trafficking and physical assault to non-payment of salary, besides others (NESCH, 2011: 24). Off and on, serious atrocities against the Northeasterners have been committed in different parts of India as well. Given the rapidity with which successive incidents of assault on people from Northeast was taking place posing serious threat to the community as a whole, it has assumed the status of a national crisis. The threats against Northeasterners are becoming a sensitive issue, as it also pertains to the issue of tolerance towards minorities in cities.

In our study, we have evolved a query where respondents are asked whether they have come across their friends or relatives being sexually molested and face physical assaults. Instead of directing the questions directly to respondent's experience, and what has happened to them, we have tried to make it more impersonal. It has been devised in such a way to ensure that respondents do not feel any inhibition to report their experiences (see Table 18).

Table 18

Accounts of Assault on Friends and Relatives

Response	*Number*	*Percentage*
Yes	49	37.98
No	79	61.24
No Response	1	0.77
Total	129	100

From the responses presented in the table, it is seen that though the number of serious atrocities that Northeast respondents experienced in the city is lesser than the number reported for simple harassments, the number is by no means insignificant. Around 37.98 per cent respondents confirmed that their friends and relatives have experienced assaults in the streets and localities in Delhi. Considering that the Northeasterners are in a minority in the city and with far smaller population in comparison to other communities, the crime rate against them turns out to be quite high. While numerous factors may be responsible for the high incidence of crime against the people of Northeast, we cannot ignore the fact that they have distinct racial feature that easily marked them out as 'different' from the dominant Indian population. Their distinctive look and lifestyle also clearly mark them out as the 'outsider' in the locality and city where they live and work. Their social position of not belonging to the place and community makes them vulnerable to physical assaults and sexual molestations.

Notwithstanding their distinctive looks, it would be naïve to view discrimination against the Northeasterner solely through the prism of race. While the forms of discrimination that Northeast migrants experienced in the city definitely contain elements of racism, the phenomenon cannot be disassociated from factors of caste, class and patriarchy. Interviews conducted with a cross section of Northeast migrants in Delhi reveal that the experience sharply diverges on the lines of ethnicity, class and gender. Whereas migrants hailing from the Barak and Brahmaputra valleys seldom encountered experience of racism, those from the hills and Imphal valley cited numerous instances of discrimination: ranging from racial slurs and comments to discrimination on wages and leave at the workplace, to excessive 'search' by security personnel placed at the entry points to places such as malls, government offices and allied establishments. A comparison of the information gathered from the interviews with those obtained through casual conversations with Northeast families, which have had long tenure of stay in Delhi and belonging to the upper strata of the occupational ladder, revealed that there is an inverse correlation between experience of discrimination, on the one hand, and social position and age of the person, on the other. In the first place, the data reveals that most of the persons who claimed that they have been subjected to 'racial'/social discrimination are the youths, primarily students who live in rented accommodation with their friends in village localities such as Munirka, Masudpur, Humayunpur, Mukherjee Nagar and like places.

This is followed by workers in the service sectors such as shops, hotels, restaurants, gyms, spas and allied activities, who lacked requisite education and employed on a casual or contractual basis with no security benefits or legal protection to their position. While most of the discriminations experienced were with respect to work-related issues, such as delayed or non-payment of salary, denial of leave, and long working hours, this category of persons are also most vulnerable to abusive treatment and violence in the streets. Data on crimes against Northeast people registered with the Delhi Police between the middle of February 2014 and first week of August 2015 shows that out of 1219 complaints received, 66 are related to salary disputes, 296 to petty quarrel and 350 to 'others'.[2]

There is also a strong gender dimension in the crimes perpetrated against the Northeasterners. Almost one fourth of the crimes registered were against women, of which 163 related to rape, molestation, eve teasing, stalking and allied acts, 135 involved theft, chain snatching, dacoity and cheating (ibid.). As noted before, the perception that Northeast women are morally loose make them easy target of attack by unscrupulous elements. In many cases the problem is reinforced by their poor economic status and restrictions of the labour market, which has pushed many women into the unregulated world of the informal sector to earn their livelihood, where they get exposed to exploitations of various types.

The facts gathered suggest that crimes against Northeasterners cannot be simplistically summed up under the rubric of racism. While we need to acknowledge that acts of racial discrimination may have taken place, all misconceptions and stereotypes towards the people from Northeast cannot be considered as racist in nature. To take accounts of actual racial discrimination, we need to identify those actions and behaviours that are specifically directed towards the physical feature, and conceptions that are dependent on colour of the skin. Viewed thus, not all criminal attacks on

Northeasterners can be wholly considered as racial hatred. Close analysis shows that most of the crimes perpetrated on the Northeasterners are the effect of a complex interplay of factors, such as caste, class, patriarchal ideology (in the context of crimes against women) and growing lawlessness in the city. However, terms of intercommunity differences have increasingly come to be defined on the basis of physiological traits and colour tone, therefore whenever people from Northeast end up as victims there have been reports of attacks on people with similar looks, but different origin. And, whenever the state attempts to control the movement of foreign nationals, such as Tibetans, the people from Northeast find themselves at the wrong end, without a fault being committed. Like all identities, racial identity also seems to have remained in a state of flux in cities across India, as it often gets conflated and contrasted with the notion of nationality and ethnicity.

Whereas the Northeasterner's oriental looks may have marked them out from the rest of the Indian population, this does not mean that they have remained the perennial 'other' in the city. An examination of the pattern of social relations in the everyday life of the Northeasterners in the city reveals that the sheer compulsion of living and working together has served to bring people of different races and cultures closer together resulting in bonds of friendship and intimate sharing of ideas and things with each other. A close look at the pattern of interaction between the Northeast respondents and their counterparts at the workplace affirms this fact.

Social and Cultural Encounters in the Workplace

Workplaces are one of those sites of intimate 'mixing' in the city, where people from various social and cultural backgrounds come together to perform a singular task and fulfil their contract. The workplace, with its hierarchical structure and maze of rules and regulations that govern the relations between employers and employees or between bosses and subordinates, is not a site of professional encounter alone but a shared space where fellow workers get to know each other from close quarters making the contact socially significant. Some of the respondents in our study have confided earlier that their colleagues are quite helpful and understanding, thus they shared healthy relationship with each other. From the formal relationships that exist in workplace, the relationship can move to a more personal level. Workplaces can shape long-term relationships between individuals and communities. There have been numerous instances where people from Northeast have married their colleagues. On the flipside, there have also been numerous cases of harassment and discrimination to people from Northeast in their workplaces. In the study conducted by Northeast Support Centre & Helpline, (2011: 24), it has been noted that few Northeast workers had not been paid their salary by the employers and harassed by the co-workers. Work places involve negotiations of various kinds, where one's cultural and racial identity can become a boon as well as bane. There have also been cases where people from Northeast are preferred over workers from other parts of the country, as their presence is seen as adding a 'global look' to the business venture. With the deepening of the liberalization process and the paradigm shift in India's foreign policy, which has resulted in a significant tilt towards Southeast Asia and the ASEAN block of countries, the Northeasterners' distinctive look and proficiency in English have made them quite popular with business houses and the corporate sector.

From the data presented in Chapter 3, it is seen that over 41 per cent of our respondents are employed, with most of them working either in the government establishments or multinational corporations and private sectors. These groups of individuals occupy a different social position in their community as well as in the social milieu of the city. The number of Northeasterners taking up employment in the city is a rising feature, and they have ventured into various sectors previously unknown to them. From the earlier trend of moving to cities and urban centres for higher studies, there is a discernible shift towards migration in search of jobs and better livelihood options. It is not only the Indian cities that have caught the fancy of Northeasterners looking for better jobs. Many of them have also gone abroad and join hospitality sectors that move to countries around the world, such as cruise liner. However, the concentrations of workers in urban centres within the country remain much higher than those going or seeking jobs in foreign countries.

The nature of work and employments of Northeast migrants can be seen from the data presented in Tables 19 and 20, furnished below:

Table 19

Employment Profile

Tenure in Years	*Number*	*Percentage*
< 2 Years	18	33.96
3 Years	9	16.98
5 Years	6	11.32
10 + Years	20	37.73
Total	53	100

Table 20

Nature of Employment

Nature	*Number*	*Percentage*
Permanent	33	62.26
Temporary	13	24.52
Contractual	7	13.20
Total	53	100

The information on the length of service put in by the employed respondents in their job reveal that the number of workers who have recently joined employment is much higher than those who have worked for 3 to 5 years, while those who have worked for more than 10 years are the highest in the group. The data indicates two significant trends of employment scenario for Northeast workers in the city. One, there is high presence of new workers, which suggests that most of them might have come to the city recently or had come to study in the city and subsequently took up employment as a means to earn and support their study. Two, those who have found employment have chosen to remain in the city for longer period in order to consolidate their career. The employed may have found working and living in the city more rewarding than going back to their home state, or moving about from place to place.

The data also reveals another significant fact that most of the respondents are engaged in permanent jobs. From the information gathered, we have come to know that most of the workers from Northeast are engaged in government jobs, which constitutes a majority (62.26%) in the group. As government jobs are usually much sought after by workers from Northeast, it is only logical that they will stick to their job rather than move to another sector or to other places in search of better avenues. This could be one of the major reasons that we see large number of workers engaged in permanent jobs. Some have opined that one aspect that might have helped workers getting permanent jobs in government establishment is reservation policy, which tribes and other reserved category from Northeast might have taken advantage of. However, as stated earlier, this cannot be seen as a general factor for all Northeast workers, as more than two-thirds of the Northeast population comprised non-tribes.

Be that as it may, the significant fact is workers from Northeast and the sectors they are joining have become more diversified with the increase in migration. What we can foresee in the future is the rise of workers engaged in temporal employment and perhaps gradual decrease among those engaged in permanent jobs. The gradual process of migration indicates that students who moved to the city for higher education usually end up staying back by taking up employment in the city as employment avenues in their home states are not very good. Therefore, workers from Northeast have been going places to get better employment opportunities, and many are willing to join any sector that will absorb them.

Interestingly, unlike the findings of the North East Support Centre & Helpline (2011: 24), which reported that the Northeast workers faced discrimination in the hands of employers, most of the workers in our study mentioned that they do not face any discrimination at the workplace or in getting leave for special occasions. It appears that the intercommunity relationship in workplaces has been cordial and convenient for our respondents. This could be one reason why many chose to remain in the city, despite some forms of hardship and discriminations that they face in other aspects of their everyday life.

Sharing of Space and Food at the Workplace

To get a better understanding of life at the workplace and the interpersonal dynamics among the workers, we have interrogated the sharing of food with colleagues at work. In India, sharing of food carries high symbolic value, where strict commensal rules based on caste regulate the exchange of food among individuals and groups. Accepting or sharing food with someone not only signifies social acceptance of the concerned person but also puts the status of the recipient at risk if his or her ritual status is higher than the giver. Though most of the respondents in the study fall outside the framework of caste, the food they eat locates them at the lower rung of the ladder vis-à-vis their mainland colleagues for whom vegetarianism carries the highest ritual and social value. Mention has already been made of the problems Northeast tenants faced with their landlords over what they eat, which has made food a perennial source of tension in intercultural relationship. Given this backdrop, sharing of food at work can be a major step towards building better understanding of and respect for cultures that differ from one's own. Hence the analysis is concerned less with what people eat, as with what happens when the formal relationship is translated into sharing and experimenting with the other's food habits.

As far as Northeast food is concerned, the workplace appears to be the perfect place for sharing it with people from other community. The sharing of food among the workers belonging to various communities, as per the findings seems to have happened without much conundrum. The sharing is taking place in a social environment where workers are known to each other through close association. Therefore, some form of respect for each other's culture and food habits seems to have developed. Although some form of antagonism and negative comments to foods that were prepared by Northeast colleagues are reported, on the whole we find wide acceptance among the peers.

It is also important to note that the act of sharing food is a mutual process that takes place on both sides of the cultural divide where Northeast workers are also being offered food that were prepared by their colleagues at an overwhelming rate. As per the responses shown in Tables 21–25, it is found that 56.60 per cent respondents shared the food they packed to work with their colleagues and 66.03 per cent of colleagues shared their food with them. To the question whether they experience any show of antagonism from their colleagues and employers over the food they consume, 73.58 per cent respondents replied in the negative as against 15.09 per cent who replied in the affirmative.

Table 21

Source of Food

Response	*Number*	*Percentage*
Brought from Home	25	47.16
Bought from Canteen	21	39.62
No Response	7	13.20

Table 22

Food Shared with Colleagues

Response	*Number*	*Percentage*
Yes	30	56.60
No	3	5.66
No Response	20	37.73

Table 23

Food Shared by Colleagues

Response	*Number*	*Percentage*
Yes	35	66.03
No	3	5.66
No Response	15	28.30

Table 24

Experience of Antagonism Towards Food Eaten

Response	*Number*	*Percentage*
Yes	8	15.09
No	39	73.58
No Response	6	11.32

Table 25

Experience of Comments on Food Eaten

Response	*Number*	*Percentage*
Yes	17	32.07
No	29	54.71
No Response	7	13.20

In comparative terms, the data indicates that the lived experience of Northeasterners at the workplace differ from the other aspects of their life in the city. In the office, the Northeast workers not only find respect, but also greater acceptance of their cultural difference, which is not easy to come by in the localities where they live.

This affective mode of interaction where intimate sharing of varied cultural practices leading to accommodation at personal and community level may be seen as, what Ayona Datta calls, 'mongrelization' of Northeastern culture in urban India.[3] We have not seen so much of close and cordial sharing of culture between people from Northeast and other communities in urban India; hostility towards each other has been the hallmark of relationships that Northeast share with other communities. However, workers from Northeast are moving places and between various sectors, thus making the inroad of their lifestyle and culture into many aspects of Indian society. The process points to a strong possibility that shared professional space can ultimately lead to wider acceptance of Northeasterners as they are, notwithstanding the deep racial and cultural distinction.

A critical question that arises at this juncture is to what extent does such cultural intermixing help in overcoming the rigid boundaries of marriage that is characteristic of all cultures? Given that marriage is both a unifying and dividing force, uniting members of the 'in-group' in close alliance while sharpening the wedge with the 'out-group', it would be pertinent to examine what effect migration and exposure to other cultures have on Northeasterner's attitude to marriage and intimacy. In the next chapter, we focus our attention on this intensely private and emotive issue.

Notes

1. NESCH, 2011. *North East Migration and Challenges in National Capital Cities*, A Research Report by North East Support Centre & Helpline, Delhi.
2. 'Problems of Northeast People in Delhi', a crime report by Robin Hibu, Joint Commissioner of Police and Nodal Officer for North East Region, presented at an Interactive Session between the Members of Parliament from the eight Northeastern states and members of the Northeast diaspora in Delhi, organized by Northeast MPs Forum and Northeast India Voluntary Society on 4 August 2015, at Constitution Club, Delhi.
3. According to Ayona Datta (2011), 'mongrelization' refers to syncretism of various cultures in enclosed social urban spaces.

C HA

Cros

Marria

In recen
matter
commun
tions in
in many
India
resentm
outside
cated o
The res
they are
also as
for a w
image o
strict c
commun

Marriag

In her c
Southeas
control
rooted

CHAPTER 5

Crossing Boundaries

Marriage and Intimacy Across Cultures

In recent times, intercommunity marriage has become a matter of grave social concern, especially among those communities that strive to maintain their custom and traditions intact. 'Honour killing'[1] has become a common feature in many parts of India, particularly in North and Northwest India (Sushani Raj, 2012). There is great amount of resentment when marriage takes place with person(s) outside the community, where the boundaries are demarcated on the basis of caste or religion (Choudhury, 2009). The resentment is particularly acute in the case of women, as they are seen not only as the property of the community but also as the repository of their culture and tradition. Hence for a woman to marry 'out' is seen as a serious dent to the image of the community. To prevent such an eventuality, strict control of women's sexuality is maintained by the community across cultures.

Marriage and the Control of Female Sexuality

In her comparative study of women and kinship in South and Southeast Asia, Leela Dube (1997) uses the concept 'corporate control' to show how the control over female sexuality is rooted in patriarchal ideology and in the consciousness of territoriality and group solidarity, which gives men the right to exercise power over women and dictate every facet of their behaviour. This ideology is not only confined to mainland India alone where patriarchy runs deep and intense, but found in other parts of the country as well, though the form and degree varies. Whether it is in rural areas or in the cities, communities put social pressure and constraints on women who attempt to establish marital relation with persons from outside the community (Kalpagam, 2008).

It is not only religion or custom(s) that determined opposition to marriage unions. There have been numerous grounds for opposing marriage by family members, even if the marital relationship remains well within acceptable parameters (Judge, 2012). In most of the communities in Northeast India, the boundaries for marriage are drawn on the lines of 'tribe' and 'religion'. To maintain the exclusivity and solidarity of the tribe, intra-tribal endogamy is strived at and marriage with outsiders strongly discouraged, even with a fellow tribal of another community.

Notwithstanding such oppositions from society, marital relationships across the social and religious divide was no stranger to communities in Northeast and continues to occur at an increasing rate. However, given the sharp opposition to marrying out, marriage becomes an interplay of love and customs, where many individuals find themselves at fault without the least intention of becoming social rebels.

People from Northeast are considered as more liberal and progressive than their counterparts in other parts of the country. Though endogamy at the level of tribe and community has been the prescribed norm for marriage in most societies of Northeast, marrying outside the fold has been a common feature from the days of yore. For instance, communities such as Khasi has had a long tradition of cross-cultural marriage, with many clans bearing the generic name 'Dkhar' or the prefix 'Khar' added to the indigenous title, as indication of their non-Khasi origin. This would imply that

Northeasterners have fairly liberal attitude towards sensitive issues or give more space to personal choices, whether it is in matters of one's career or marriage.

This, however, is not the case everywhere, nor is the situation the same at all points of time. When there is a strong force of political assertion of identity, we can expect some forms of restraint towards intercommunity marriage. Besides, what are the actual boundaries being demarcated for marital relationships may be ambiguous, as a Naga tribe may oppose his sister marrying another Naga from a different community. Hence the issue cannot be generalized but needs to be continuously tested by facts on the ground. The analysis here is an attempt to assess how far Northeasterners live up to their reputation as an open and accommodative community, and how individuals would react to a social situation where there is crossing of community boundary and intermixing of race and culture in marital relationships.

Boy–Girl Relationship Outside the Community

In the course of social interaction, the probability of forging friendly ties and close relations with persons of the other gender from outside the community for settlers in the cities is fairly high. Unless and until the individual or community is too cocooned within its own social milieu, friendship with the 'other', from every side of the group, is socially inevitable. People of Northeast living in Delhi have also made their presence felt in every social circle, moving in and out of their community with apparent ease. Their openness, however, has not gone down well with the orthodox; and many have had to face the ire of critics, both from within and outside the group, for their supposed lack of loyalty to the community (see also Nongbri, 2003: 229–267).

The analysis of answers on the issue of intercommunity intimacy, posed in the questionnaire, reveals that most of the respondents are not willing to share information about their status of relationship with the opposite gender from outside the community. From the data presented in Table 26 it is seen that 46.51 per cent gave a blank answer to the query. The figure indicates that although they have moved to the city, such relationship remains a sensitive issue for many of the individuals and communities from Northeast India. Only a little of over a tenth (10.85%) of respondents admitted that they share close relationship with a boy or girl outside their community. Interestingly, the negative answers are also much higher than the positive ones, which suggest that people from Northeast are not inclined to have close relationship with persons of the opposite gender from other communities.

Table 26

Account of Inter-Community Intimate Relations

Response	*Number*	*Percentage*
Yes	14	10.85
No	55	42.63
No Response	60	46.51
Total	129	100

The reasons cited by the respondents for their unwillingness to enter into intercommunity relationship bring to the fore not only personal preferences, but also the socio-cultural barriers and stereotypes about the so-called other. Some of the reasons given by the respondents for not getting into intimate relationship plainly show the deep trust-deficit that characterizes the relations between the Northeasterner and members of the dominant community. Some of the answers bluntly state: *'Never trust them that much to become best friends'*, and *'I just don't want to have close relationship with them'*. Many respondents have also simply stated *'Not interested'* to establish intimate relationship with the opposite gender from outside the community. For many Northeasterners, this appears to be a personal choice that has been decided from the initial period of their arrival in the city that they were not going to cultivate such types of relationship with the opposite sex outside the community. Prominent among the reasons given by the respondents for not getting involved in such relationship stemmed from the perception that there are irreconcilable religious and cultural differences between them that could unsettle the relationship. Some respondents plainly expressed that there are *'Differences and incompatibilities of culture, lifestyle, eating habits, etc.'* that are difficult to resolve. Hence, accommodation of each other's culture became the ultimate barrier for some.

The varied reasons cited by the respondents for their reluctance to get into serious relationships with the other gender from outside their community show that most Northeasterners in Delhi are not ready to embrace the cultural 'other' in their private life. But while many want to remain within the confine of their own community for marriage and intimate relations, they do not mind friendship with persons from other communities within the limit of distant relations. Thus, at the level of friendship, we find that the respondents are much more forthcoming, not only in sharing information but also in establishing close relations with persons of the same gender from other communities. However, the same responses have not been seen with respect to persons of the other gender.

Probing deeper into the issue bring to the fore that many Northeasterners are also averse to establishing close relations with the opposite gender outside their community due to the misconceived ideas the 'other' generally carry about their morality. Answering to our query on the issue, a student from Manipur categorically replied, *Indian boys do not understand the meaning of platonic friendship. In their perception, friendly gesture by a girl means they want to get intimate. What is more, the poor opinion 'mainstream' people generally have of our character make many of us wary to have any close relations with them, beyond the bare essential.*

Attitude towards Interethnic and Interreligious Marriage

Notwithstanding the strong reservations shown by the individuals in our sample towards intimate relations with the cultural 'other', marriage between Northeasterners and people from other parts of India is gradually increasing not only in the cities into which they have come as students and workers, but also back home with long time settlers in the region or recent newcomers to the area for business and employment. To gauge the attitude of the Northeasterners to this development, we asked our respondents to give their views on interethnic and interreligious marriage. Interestingly, most of the respondents stated that they do not see any problem in having intercommunity marriage as long as the individuals involved are able to adjust and cooperate with each other. In the words of one respondent: *Its okay as long as they can manage and cooperate with each other.*

Though endogamy at the level of tribe and community continues to be the norm and an ideal form of marriage for most, marriage is increasingly seen as a personal affair especially among the educated. Many respondents expressed the view that marriage is an act that should be left to the individuals concerned, a matter that others should not interfere with or impose their will on. Marriage is seen as something that evolves from emotional bonding and understanding arrived at between two individuals. Hence, society and social differences should not come in the way. Most do not seem to care as long as intercommunity marriage happens to other persons, whether they are from their community or not.

The matter takes a different turn when we examine the answers of our respondents towards interreligious marriage. Most of the respondents who responded to the query look at 'interethnic' and 'interreligious' marriage in different light. While many are quite open and do not seem to have much problem with interethnic marriage, the attitude towards interreligious marriage is quite the reverse. There are few supporters for interreligious marriage either with respect to themselves or for others. In the words of some of the respondents:

> I'm okay with interethnic, but not with interreligious marriage, since religion is a sensitive issue.
>
> Interethnic marriage is fine as long as they are cultured people. But I don't really encourage interreligious marriage, it goes against my belief.
>
> No problem with interethnic marriage. But I do not feel comfortable with interreligious marriage.

From the views expressed, it is evident that the respondents are quite clear in their mind about the difference in the two types of marriage and the consequences they entail for the parties involved. In a comment specifically directed at interreligious marriage, a respondent from the predominantly Christian state of Nagaland wrote: *According to me, it will not work out because a person who truly believes in God will not marry someone who does not believe in God.* Such view and the associated classification of persons and groups into 'believers' and 'non-believers' reflected in the above comment not only brings to the fore the wide gulf that characterizes the relations between the Northeast migrants and the dominant population, but also betrays elements of religious fundamentalism that considers other forms of beliefs and practices inferior to one's own. According to such stand, marital union between two individuals from different religious backgrounds will only be an act of sacrilege, and which has to be opposed by all means.

Echoing the same line of thought, a respondent from Meghalaya notes: *Strongly opposed interreligious marriage because I cannot compromise the way I believe in God. I will have no problem if the person is a Christian.* Here again, we find religion is the sole criterion that makes a person eligible for marriage. One does not see much concern for personal quality, race, class, ethnic background or nationality of the prospective spouse, but religion is all that matters for consideration of marital relations. This attitude clearly suggests that it is not only difference in language, culture and race that stifle the growth of cordial intercommunity relationships, but religious differences may actually be a significant factor that makes the divide irreconcilable as well. While it would be presumptuous to assume that all Northeasterners subscribe to such an orthodox position, the presence of individuals who support such rigid social codes do not bode well for intercommunity relations.

To arrive at a meaningful understanding of what made our respondents to adopt differential valuation of interethnic and interreligious marriage, it would be instructive to step back and take a close look at the social background of our respondents and the activities they engaged in as members of the community, which is discussed earlier in the study. Though the sample has not been disaggregated by religion, from the information presented in Chapter 3, it is revealed that 74.4 per cent respondents regularly attend community-based church service and fellowships, which clearly suggests that many of them are followers of Christianity, a belief that is at sharp variance, doctrinally and ritualistically, with most of the Indian belief systems.

It would be prudent to note that it is not Christianity *per se*, but the way in which the faith is practiced by the Northeast community, in particular, and Christian migrants in general, in the cities they migrate to that shape the attitude and worldview of its members. Dislocated from their habitat and traditional support structure, for most migrants the church plays an important role as a surrogate mother and support system that is critical for survival in an alien environment. In such a milieu, interreligious marriage would be most incompatible; it would interfere not only with the members' belief but also with their lived reality, which basically revolves round the church and community of believers. Hence, while many respondents see nothing wrong with interethnic marriage, if the parties involved belong to the same faith, they are not willing to accept interreligious marriage as this would be highly disruptive not only to their religious beliefs and practices but also of the socio-cultural order within which they are embedded. This fear of upsetting the socio-cultural and socio-religious order lies at the root of religious conservatism among the Northeasterners, which is not generally seen in other aspects of their life. Marriage thus becomes not only a crucial factor for upholding their particular form of belief and life ways, but also the ultimate test of loyalty to the group.

Needless to say, marriage remains a contentions terrain in so far as intercommunity relationships are concerned. It is not only among the people of Northeast, but similar attitudes and perceptions towards intercultural unions are found in societies of other parts of India as well. It is where personal choice and societal norms and constraints come together to determine what action an individual takes that could have serious effect on cross-cultural relations. More significantly, the city has remained an arena where such actions are materialized, and extensive interactions between various cultures and race take place. It is in the city that unions are forged and identities concretely formed or transformed, negotiated and renegotiated with varied social actors and situations.

Note

1. Paramjit Judge has defined 'honour killing' as 'young lovers murdered usually by the girl's kin to uphold family honour' (2012: 44).

CHAPTER 6

State and Civil Society Response

Amidst the deep cultural gulf that characterizes the relations between the people of Northeast and the dominant population, the two communities have been able to strike a working relationship with each other without much ado to disrupt the even tenor of everyday life. However, increasing crime against persons of Northeast origin and continuing state and public apathy to the problem has deepened the sense of insecurity in the Northerners and fomented growing unhappiness with the state and its law enforcing agencies at the callous indifference to their problem: complaints made do not get registered; of those that are, proper investigations are not conducted and judicial hearings delayed, allowing criminals to escape scot-free even in 'open and shut' cases. The situation has further been complicated by the absence of effective laws to try offences against Northerners, many of which fall in the category of 'hate crime' triggered by racial prejudice and xenophobia.

We have been cautious in our approach and shied away from the tendency that looks at crimes against Northeasterners solely through the lens of race. Since many factors may be at work in the perpetration of crime labelling an offence as 'racist' without concrete evidence to support the claim could end up defeating the very cause of justice. While we reiterate our stand on the issue and argue for the need to look at things in a more nuanced and holistic fashion, increasing incidence and peculiar pattern of violence inflicted on people from the region have lent weight to the popular view that there are strong racial elements in the attack on Northerners. However, the state and the ruling class in the country have never admitted that racism is an issue in India. Unlike many countries in the West where proper mechanisms are in place to tackle racism, India's state of denial has directly and indirectly aided perpetrators of such crime to get away with impunity.

The 'Turning Point', Bezbaruah Committee and Measures for Remedy

The death of Nido Tania on 29 January 2014 marked a turning point in the state's approach to the Northeast issue. The tragic circumstances that led to his death and the unhappy coincidence that it came as a sequel to a series of violence and loss of valuable lives in different parts of the country ignited fiery reactions across diverse segments of the Northeast community. Backed by a sympathetic media and rights-based groups, mass protests by students, activists and civil society organizations erupted in several cities and towns calling for immediate and effective action by the government to put an end to the discrimination and violence against the people of Northeast. The scale of the protests and the public anger the case generated forced the Central Government to set up a special committee under the chairmanship of Shri M.P. Bezbaruah, a retired Indian Administrative Service (IAS) officer, to look into the issue and suggest appropriate measures that could be taken up by the government for immediate action. The committee, which comprised mainly senior bureaucrats with requisite experience on Northeast affairs,[1] was given two months to complete its report on the following terms of reference:

1. To examine the various kinds of concerns, including security of the persons hailing from the Northeastern states.
2. To examine the causes behind attacks/violence and discrimination against the people of the Northeastern states.
3. To suggest measures to be taken by the government to address the concerns.
4. To suggest legal remedies to address these concerns (GOI, 2014).[2]

After series of consultations with diverse groups of people from Northeast residing in different cities[3] and belonging to different walks of life: activists, academicians, members of the legal fraternity and other professional bodies, students and civil society organizations, the committee compiled its report and submitted the same to the Ministry of Home Affairs, Government of India, in February 2015.[4]

Northeast representatives with members of the Bezbaruah Committee

(Photograph courtesy: Mavio Woiba)

Taking serious note of the often-repeated question raised by critics, *why special measures are needed for the Northeast people as such reprehensible incidents are part of metro life and other citizens too faced such problems* (GOI, 2014: 5, italics added), the committee began its report by citing four interrelated reasons to justify why special steps are called for:

(i) The proportionately high number of incidents involving the people from the Northeast in comparison to their population in Delhi.

(ii) The rising number of incidents of racial nature, molestation, prejudices, specially directed towards Northeast communities has led to widespread perception among the people that they are particularly targeted for reason of their distinct physical feature.

(iii) Because of such incidents, a large number of youths from the region grow up in the capital with negative feelings. Their widespread experience of being subjected to taunts, humiliation and racial attacks in the capital city and other metros make them feel bitter, angry and frustrated.

(iv) The most worrisome is the rippling effect that such experiences have on the region, which is already witnessing separatist movements and strong feeling of alienation among the youth. The feeling that the authorities are apathetic to such concerns aggravates such tendencies (GOI, 2014).

Seized of the above-stated problem, the committee concentrated on five 'components' in its deliberations to work out actionable measures for speedy resolution of the problem. These include law, law enforcement and investigation, support system for victims, justice delivery, and socio-economic and cultural initiatives (GOI, 2014: 15). Working on each component, the committee came up with wide ranging recommendations that called for appropriate and timely action by different organs of the state machinery and civil society. Based on the urgency and time frame for implementation, the recommendations are classified into three distinct categories: 'immediate', 'short term' and 'long term', ranging from 6 months to 1 year, 1 year to 18 months, and 18 months to 2 years, respectively.

Prominent among the recommendations made are amendment of existing laws and/or enactment of a new law to make crime against Northeast people cognizable, nonbailable and punishable in the court of law; completion of investigations in 60 days and trial in 90 days; *creation of Fast Track Courts for handling cases relating to North East people, particularly those which are racially motivated and heinous crimes against North East women and children* (emphasis in original, GOI, 2014: 31–32); creation of a Special Police Unit for the North Eastern Region (SPUNER) having the power of a police station and jurisdiction over whole of Delhi; appointment of a Nodal Officer at Police Headquarters to oversee all cases relating to Northeast and coordinate with the eight Northeastern states for recruitment of personnel from the respective states in Delhi Police. These measures are deemed vital to strengthen the law enforcement machinery and instil confidence in Northeast people, many of who experienced harrowing time to get complaints registered with the local police. Other recommendations include investigation of cases should be carried out by a special squad headed by an officer not below the rank of DSP[5] or ACP[6]; appointment of special prosecutors to handle cases of atrocities against people of Northeast; recruitment of advocates from Northeast to assist in the disposal of cases; formation of a panel of lawyers, preferably from Northeast with women constituting 50 per cent of the panel, for provision of legal aid to members of Northeast community; synchronize Special Helpline number 1093 for Northeast youth with 100, the Police Control Room number so that complaints of Northeast people may be directly brought to the notice of DCP/SPUWC[7] and Chief Coordinator for Northeast.

Besides the range of administrative and legal measures identified for action by the state, the committee also laid strong emphasis on the importance of sensitization as a means to generate awareness and infuse spirit of tolerance and mutual respect for the socially and culturally different. To realize this objective, the committee proposes cultural exchange programmes for schools and college students, sensitization of the security forces and public service providers at the grassroots level, use of sports to educate and foster mutual bond and understanding among people, and establishment of a North East Centre in Delhi to enhance visibility of the region and its rich culture and tradition. Special emphasis has also been placed on the role of cultural centres, universities and the mass media (both national and regional) to disseminate information on diverse aspects of the region and promote its integration with the nation.

The committee also calls upon all State Bhawans of the Northeastern states located in the city to take extra steps to minimize the problems faced by the people by informing and educating newcomers from their respective states on the various legal and social requirements relating to accommodation, employment, educational and hospital admissions, modes of transport, general safety and relief, and so forth.

Implementation Dynamics: Gulf between Action and Promise

If we were to go by the scope of the recommendations made by the Bezbaruah Committee, one would expect that the problems faced by the Northeasterner would soon be a thing of the past. However, as the cliché 'there's a slip between the cup and the lips' goes, there is a wide gap between action and promise. Except for some notable achievements in the police department such as appointment of a nodal officer to look into the grievances of Northeast people, establishment of a Special Police Unit for the Northeastern Region and allotment of a 1.2 acres of prime land for the same at Nanakpura* (an upmarket neighbourhood close to the elite localities of Santiniketan and

* Personal Communication, Robin Hibu.

Vasant Vihar in South Delhi), most of the recommendations have remained largely on paper. While the slow pace of progress could be due to a variety of factors, lack of coordination among the different implementing agencies seems to be a major stumbling block, a fact that came to the fore at a recent meeting called by the North East MP's Forum and North East India Welfare Society (a Delhi-based NGO run by Northeast activists) to deliberate on the outcomes of the report and related issues. Though the recommendations made by the Bezbaruah Committee fall under the purview of different ministries, and clearly specified as such in its report, in his address to the participants at the above-mentioned meeting, the Union Minister of State for Home made it clear that the implementation and monitoring of the recommendations lies with the Home Ministry.[8] Also, appeals made by Northeast representatives for the formation of a monitoring committee to keep track of and expedite actions on the recommendations met with little response from the government.

A close examination of the actions taken on the report thus far suggests that the government sees the Northeast issue primarily as a law and order problem, which can be resolved by increasing the strength of the law enforcement agency and improvement in its performance. In what is indicative of this line of thinking, Robin Hibu, a decorated and highly respected Indian Police Service officer from Arunachal Pradesh and the newly appointed Nodal Officer for the Northeastern region in Delhi, proudly informed a group of Northeast activists of the government's massive drive to recruit police personnel from the Northeastern states and hire volunteers from among Northeast youth to assist the police and serve as a bridge between the department and the community. It was revealed and plan was also in the offing to purchase a fleet of patrol vehicles, which would be manned by personnel from the Special Northeast Unit and carrying its own name and crest to keep watch on Northeast populated localities. This, according to Hibu, will not only counter crime against the Northeasterners but will also serve to instil confidence in them.[9] To what extent Hibu's enthusiasm and seriousness of purpose will translate into tangible gains for the Northeasterners is a moot point, but what goes to the credit of the officer and his office is that the same seriousness is not seen in other departments.

This is not to suggest that nothing is happening in other departments. It would be a travesty of facts if we fail to acknowledge the measures taken by the Ministry for Development of Northeastern Region (MoDONER) with respect to the matter. In an apparent bid to project its concern for the Northeasterners and win over the youth, the ministry has come up with a number of activities such as observation of social awareness week, vigilance week, cultural programmes and interactive sessions with students and activists.

While such steps are seen as important means to bring the people and the law makers together for effective resolution of the problem, some of the events attended by the first author suggest that they are more in the nature of crisis management strategies to tide over the situation than carefully planned exercise for constructive and long-term gains. A college student from Assam whom the author spoke to at one of the events organized by the Ministry dismissed it as a propaganda designed to secure the Northeasterners' support for the party in power. Another student, a girl from Manipur was irked that nothing comes out of these events. She states, 'The promises the politicians make or the suggestions we give never see the light of day but buried under the bane of bureaucratic red-tapism'. Echoing a similar point of view, a senior activist who has been part of several teams that engaged in negotiations with the government, expressed his concern at the poor response shown by the officials. Many are also upset with the government for its failure to rein in employers in the unorganized sectors who defraud Northeast employees of their wages, hours of work and other social security benefits by refusing to comply with prescribed labour laws. The problem is worse for women employees, as many employers blatantly flout the Sexual Harassment of

Women at Workplace Act on women's safety, exposing the workers to sexual harassment and exploitations of various kinds. Among the most vulnerable are girls who work at call centres, business firms and massage parlours, dubbed as spas. Commenting on the issue, a lady advocate expressed her dismay that the state seems to be in no hurry to bring about the much talked reforms.

A sore point for most Northeasterners is the slow pace of progress in the legal redressal mechanism. The absence of laws through which criminals can be brought to book, and loopholes in existing laws and judicial procedure, has resulted in the denial of justice to many victims. Most of the cases of murder and homicide of Northeast people registered with the Delhi police remain unsolved. Adding concern to dismay, in many of the cases the accused freely roam the streets on bail free to tamper with evidence and free to strike at other victims. According to information shared by Robin Hibu, out of 550 cases registered with Delhi Police between February 2014 and August 2015, investigations had yet to be carried out in 384 cases, 109 awaiting for trial and only in 5 cases have convictions been made.[10]

There is also little action seen on the committee's recommendation to extend relief and support to the victims of crimes and violence. Changme Sangma, a young woman from Meghalaya who works as a volunteer for Delhi Police, stated that most of the time they had to shell out money from their pockets to help families in distress meet the cost of transport and medicine. Alana Golmei who runs the North East Support Centre & Helpline reported that, short of fund and manpower, they literally have to squeeze out all their resources to rally support and meet the daily calls for help from victims and witnesses, who increasingly turn to them in times of crisis. It is also significant that most of the individuals we spoke to stated that they would rather approach the Northeast Helpline or other community support system, such as the church and students' organizations for help than the Delhi

Police. This not only raises pertinent questions about the credibility of the police and the government's commitment to implement the recommendations and resolve the problem, but also places the onus squarely on the community to come to the aid of their members in times of distress.

From Victims to Citizens: Mobilization and Assertion of Right

A significant outcome of this state of affairs is the paradigm shift in the way in which Northeasterners perceive themselves and their place in the city. Faced with the realization that the only way to protect themselves is to garner all their resources, Northeasterners are slowly coming out of their sense of 'victimhood' devoid of agency to assert their role as 'citizens' equipped with democratic rights guaranteed by the Constitution. Backed by numbers and the consciousness that their electoral choice can swing the fortune of political parties at the hustings, Northeasterners are slowly turning their disadvantage into an opportunity by redefining their rights as citizens and stakeholders in the city. In a significant development, 20 Northeast organizations came together to submit a 27-point memorandum to the Delhi Government, shortly after the Aam Aadmi Party came to power, demanding concerted action by the newly formed government for resolution of their problems.

Among the numerous demands made are appointment of one senior welfare officer under the Chief Minister's Cell headed by a senior officer preferably from Northeast who would be mandated to hold meeting once in a month with Northeast students, NGOs, social activists, government servants and state Bhawans to thrash out critical issues; nomination of one Northeast representative in Delhi State Assembly with extraordinary ordinance or legislation; appointment of one member from Northeast at Delhi Commission for Women and appointment of one member each at Delhi Minority Commission and Delhi State Consumer Disputes Redressal Commission from Northeast community.

Though the memorandum is sketchily drafted, the content clearly reflects the aspirations of a people long viewed as the social and cultural 'other' to create a legitimate space for themselves in India's capital city (see the letter in Annexure 2).

Northeast activists with Arvind Kejriwal, Chief Minister of Delhi

(Photograph courtesy: Maivo Woiba)

On a parallel plane, Northeast women activists have been actively negotiating with the Delhi Commission for Women to set up a Northeast monitoring cell in the commission to look into and expedite disposal of cases of discrimination and violence against Northeast women. In an interactive session with Ms. Swati Maliwal, DCW chairperson at Jawaharlal Nehru University, Northeast students and activists shared their concerns at the growing discrimination and violence against persons of Northeast and presented a list of demands for the Commission and state government to act upon.[11] Organizations such as North East India Welfare Society, North East Support Centre & Helpline and North East India Forum Against Racism have also been actively involved in taking up different issues affecting the community directly with concerned departments in the Union Government as well as office of the Lieutenant Governor.[12]

A significant outcome of the overt and covert negotiations carried out by Northeast activists and professionals is the constitution of the North-East India Support and Monitoring Cell (NEISMC) by Delhi Government in December 2015. The cell, which comprised 12 full members and three special invitees hailing from different Northeastern states and professional streams, is intended to aid the officials to come up with appropriate policies and implementation strategies to resolve the problems faced by Northeast migrants in the city. Whether this will translate into tangible gains and/or result in true freedom from discrimination for the Northeasterners, time alone will tell. Suffice it to say while the Delhi Government has

Ms. Swati Maliwal, Chairperson Delhi Commission for Women addressing NE students at an interactive session in JNU

been quick to respond to the demands made by the people of Northeast, the Central Government has been dragging its feet on the matter.

Participants at the session sharing their concerns on the plight of Northeasterners in the city

Expressing strong displeasure at the lackadaisical approach, the Supreme Court came down heavily on the Centre for its failure to evolve proper mechanisms to address the issue. While responding to a petition filed by Karma Dorjee, shortly after the death of Nido Tania, two years ago the Court took special note of the lack of a nodal agency to implement the recommendations made by the Bezbaruah Committee to tackle issues of hate crimes and racial abuse against the people of Northeast residing in Delhi and other cities. Terming the Centre's affidavit submitted by the Additional Solicitor General as inadequate and broad-based, the bench headed by Chief Justice T.S. Thakur observed: '[T]his is a sensitive issue which requires a proactive monitoring and corrective measures for years. There should be a nodal body to coordinate the efforts. To ask a huge amorphous body like the government to do it may not yield proper results. The court should be able to hold some one responsible for non-implementation of the devised strategy (*TOI*, 19 October 2016).[13] In the resumed hearing of the case on 21 October 2016, the apex Court granted one week's time to the Central Government 'to inform it about the proposal to set up a nodal agency to coordinate on the issue of hate crimes and racial violence, especially against the people of Northeast living in other states' (*The Hindu,* 22 October 2016).[14]

Facts on the ground indicate that Northeasterners are also slowly discovering the power of legal mechanisms, such as the Right to Information (RTI) Act and Public Interest Litigation (PIL) to secure their interests. In the words of one activist, 'in a democracy, the only way you can get things done is through public pressure and the judiciary'. However, the slowness of the due process of law and the exorbitant cost of litigation act as major deterrence for many to approach the judicial machinery. Affirming this viewpoint, Liyi Noshi[15] a Delhi-based advocate from Arunachal Pradesh states, 'justice is not cheap, in India you have to invest a lot of your time and money to get justice'; requirements that few Northeasterners seem to possess. It is, perhaps, to overcome such drawbacks that persons such as Alana Golmei who runs the North East

Support Centre & Helpline and has a Ph.D. in Political Science from Manipur University and a former Post-Doctoral fellow at Jawaharlal Nehru University has joined the LLB programme at Delhi University. Golmei has also filed a PIL in the Indian Supreme Court on the government's implementation of the recommendations made by the Bezbaruah Committee, besides actively assisting victims of crime and violence to pursue their case with the police and the courts. Attempts such as this, however, are just a drop in the ocean with the large majority languishing in helplessness, for want of tactical support. Many activists involved in the issue have expressed concern at the people's legal ignorance and lack of resources to pursue a case to its logical conclusion.

Social Media as a Tool in the Struggle

If the law has been painfully slow to deliver justice to the afflicted, revolution in information technology has provided Northeasterners with a handy tool to air their grievances and mobilize support for their cause. Like most people in the country today, Northeasterners have taken to social media in a big way. Social networking sites such as Facebook, WhatsApp and Twitter and instant SMSs and e-mails have been extensively used to share information about crimes and other occurrences in different parts of the country. The wide reach of the medium and the power of information technology to capture, and to transmit and re-transmit 'live' occurrences of events, has served as effective means to keep the struggle alive among people with democratic aspirations across social, cultural and geographical boundaries. This has not only led to new forms of political participation but also created democratic space where people openly dissect, debate and interrogate happenings in the country and the role of the government in tackling these. The Bezbaruah Committee itself would not have come into existence had it not been for the widespread outpouring of anguish and concern, circulated through the digital network, in the aftermath of Nido Tania's

Facebook picture of all faith prayer meeting at Jantar Mantar in memory of Nido Tania

death at the violence inflicted on the people of Northeast, forcing the government to take necessary action to mitigate the situation.

It is not people alone who have become avid users of social media to exchange news and views and to stay connected with one another, defying the physical constraints in interaction imposed by distance. The medium has also been put to effective use by the police who are turning to social networking sites such as Facebook and WhatsApp for regular update on crimes and other measures adopted by the agency. In a bid to reach out to the Northeasterners and elicit their cooperation for solution of the problem, the SPUNER has set up its own Facebook page and WhatsApp group where members can directly interact with the police and with each other to deliberate on issues affecting the community. At the first meeting of the newly constituted North-East India Support and Monitoring Cell (NEISMC) by the Delhi Government with the Social Welfare Minister, Advisor to the Chief Minister and officials at the Delhi Secretariat on 16 June 2016, Nodal Officer for North-East Robin

Meeting of newly constituted NEI Support and Monitoring Cell with officials of Delhi Government

(Photograph courtesy: *SPUNER*, Delhi)

Hibu described social media as the 'Lifeline of Northeast People' and informed the members that since his department set up the Northeast Facebook page in 2015, he has been contacted by over 8 million (89 lakh) Facebook users across the globe on the Northeast issue.

Intellectual Response

Exposure to the city with its numerous educational institutions and centres of learning has also triggered a surge in intellectual activity among the Northeasterners, through which they not only challenge established views but also question the historical absence of the Northeastern region in Indian standard texts and the curriculum of schools and universities: an omission that has contributed in no small way to the otherness and distorted understanding of its people in the cities. This intellectual drive can be seen operating on different modes, ranging from scholarly works in the academia, to articles in newspapers and magazines, to blogs and comments on the Internet. While many of the works had their origin in the region, a sizable chunk are authored by out-based[16] scholars located in cities, whose exposure to the exclusionary and hegemonic practices of the dominant groups lent a critical edge to their work. The growing interest in Northeast studies that swept mainland universities in the wake of increasing violence against people of the region significantly aided the process. This has provided scholars from the region a vantage point not only to critically examine emerging issues, but also to test prevailing theories and perspectives with facts on the ground. However, unlike Dalit studies, which derived their impetus mainly from the oppressive ideology and practices of Brahminic Hinduism and the inspiration of Dalit reformers and saints, resulting in a formidable body of works that is hard to contest or compete with, Northeast study remains a highly fragmented field that is reflective both of the nascent stage of the movement (if one may call it that) and heterogeneity of the universe.

Literature on the Northeast is not only divided on disciplinary lines but also bears the imprint of the ethnic and regional divisions in the society, with different groups actively engaged in the production of works relating to their community. As seen in the context of students' organizations discussed earlier, each tribe or community has its own study circle or research forum where the members regularly meet to discuss their work and allied issues pertinent to the group. Such activities however are not without their own risks, as experience from Dalit studies tells us. Kumar reveals how the Dalit literary movement, which came up as a response to the cognitive blackout of their history and culture in mainstream writings, met with strong opposition from mainstream scholars who 'discarded the Dalit literature as propagandistic, univocal and negative' hence lacking in scientific value (2010: 126).[17] Such views are no stranger to Northeast studies. In a recent conference on the region organized by a leading university in Delhi, some participants came out strongly against the tendency of Northeast scholars to work on their own society, deriding the works as of little value and demanded that UGC and ICSSR should not fund such studies. What the critics, perhaps, failed to note is that engagement with subjects or issues that affect the 'self' provides a good starting point for indepth research. Indeed, some of the celebrated texts in Indian Sociology (Srinivas, 1952; Madan, 1965/1989; Viswanathan, 1993; Robinson, 1998, 2003) are products of research carried out on one's own society by the illustrious scholars. Similarly, the huge body of knowledge created by Indian historians on subjects such as 'nationalism' and 'secularism' would not have come about had not Indian academics engaged on issues that affect the Indian 'self' as an extension of the anti-colonial struggle.

It would be no exaggeration to say that some of the respondents in our study are budding intellectuals, who judiciously combined the ideas of master theoreticians learned in the classroom with their own experiential knowledge shaped by the lived reality to engage with issues in theoretically meaningful ways through research papers, interjection at seminars, and publications in books, journals and newspapers, providing new insights and understanding to the complex mosaic that constitutes India's Northeast.

In a sharp departure from the conventional form of scholarship that stressed on value neutrality and the strict separation between research and activism, the genre of writings produced on Northeast India today – particularly by scholars located in metropolitan universities, such as Jawaharlal Nehru University, University of Delhi, Jamia Millia Islamia and Central University of Hyderabad, where there is a significant presence of students and faculty from the region – indicates the narrowing of distance between the academia and the public sphere. Northeast scholars are increasingly using the craft of their profession to question not only prejudicial stereotypes in the construction of their identity, but also the appropriateness of laws and policies adopted by the state with respect to the region. A recurrent theme that finds its echo in conference rooms and writings on Northeast India, which has a direct bearing on the subject focused in this book, is the militarization of the region and enforcement of draconian laws, such as the Armed Forces Special Powers Act (AFSPA), 1958, supposedly to maintain peace and secure its borders from external aggression. Paradoxically, far from ushering peace, the continuing enforcement of AFSPA in parts of Northeast India for over five and half decades combined with the colonially derived conceptualization of the region as a frontier that is steeped in backwardness and conflict, has not only hit normal life and posed serious obstacles to development, but also majorly contributed to the large exodus of people into the cities to escape from its tentacles and search for social, physical and economic security.

In more recent times, scholars have come out strongly against what is described as the 'state of exception'[18] in the conceptualization of Northeast which has given the state the 'legitimacy' not only to suspend normal laws but also to promote racially divisive policies. To counter the regressive approach and continuing marginalization of the region and its people in both physical and cognitive terms, Northeast scholars are seeking to redefine and reframe the region's place in the nation. In a clear move in this direction, a number of seminars and conferences dedicated to this cause have been organized in different institutions to deliberate on the issue.

It remains to be seen to what extent the growing body of works on India's Northeast witnessed today will succeed to correct the distortions inflicted on the region's culture, identity and society by insensitive stereotypes in the popular imagination of the nation, or help to reverse the process of marginalization and discrimination of the kind exposed in this study. Be that as it may, whether results can be achieved in the real world is a moot point, what is significant is the way in which Northeasterners are increasingly turning to literature (among other means) not only to register their protests at the injustice heaped upon them, but also to counter the culture of silence and hegemonic tendencies of the dominant groups, which has consigned the region, its people and their rich culture and tradition to near oblivion. It would not be an exaggeration to say, if there is a silver lining to the discrimination experienced by the people of Northeast in India's metropolitan cities today, it has not only sharpened their political consciousness but also, and more importantly, whet their appetite for learning and writing. A cursory examination of contemporary literature on the region reveals a rich mix of writings: creative, political and research-based informed by different theoretical and ideological orientations. As if, aware of the idea that 'knowledge is power' (Foucault, 1978; Bourdieu, 1991),[19] Northesterners are entering the literary world in a major way in both English and the vernacular. Aided by the proliferation of publishing houses and the catalytic role played by state-run institutions such as the University Grants Commission (UGC), Indian Council for Social Sciences Research (ICSSR), Indian Council for Historical Research (ICHR) and Sahitya Academy in the promotion of research and creative writings, one can see the birth of many insightful works that would otherwise have remained unwritten. An important consequence of this process is that this has provided the people with a platform not only to air their views but also to establish a dialogue with fellow scholars and writers across the cultural, regional and national divide, paving way for forging of solidarities and building bridges of understanding between like-minded persons.[20] Though the scale may be small, this development is critical if Northeast studies is to come out of its provincial identity as a narrow, area-bound field of study and catapult to a cosmopolitan discipline in consonance with the changing dynamics within the region and outward movement of its population.

Notes

1. In addition to the five original members who constitute the core group of the Committee, the chairman was authorized to co-opt additional members one each from the other North-eastern states not represented in the committee, namely Tripura, Mizoram and Sikkim, as well as one lady member and Shri Robin Hibu, an Indian Police Service officer and Joint Commissioner of Police, Delhi, to assist the committee in its tasks of fact finding and preparation of the report.
2. Order No. 11012/110/2012-NE-IV, dated 5.1.2014, Ministry of Home Affairs, North East Division, Government of India.
3. Apart from several meetings with activists, students' groups, academicians and civil society organizations representing different communities and states of the Northeastern region in Delhi, a city that witnessed the highest crime against Northeasterners, subgroups of the committee also visited Hyderabad, Pune and Mumbai for similar interactions with the Northeast community residing in these cities. To enable concerned individuals and groups with who direct contact could not be established to send their suggestions to the committee, a special e-mail account, namely, mbpcom.northeast@gmail.com was opened.

4. MP Bezbaruah, Report of the committee to look into the concerns of the people of the Northeast living in other parts of the country, Government of India, 2015.
5. Deputy Superintendent of Police.
6. Assistant Commissioner of Police.
7. Deputy Commissioner of Police/Special Unit for Women and Children.
8. Shri Kiren Rijiju, MOS (Home), Concluding address to the session 'Discussion on Bezbaruah Committee Recommendations' at North East MP's Forum 2015 Interactive Session, Constitution Club, Rafi Marg, New Delhi, 4 August 2015.
9. The first author's observation at a meeting with Northeast activists called by the officer on 20 August 2015. See also, 'Arunachalees Stand up for Northeast' by Special Correspondent, *Nagaland Post*, 12 October 2015, accessed on 26 October 2015.
10. Robin Hibu, 'Problems of North East People in Delhi', presented at an Interactive Session with the Members of Parliament from the Eight Northeastern states, organized by North East MPs Forum and Northeast India Welfare Society on 4 August 2015, at Constitution Club, Delhi.
11. For more on this initiative, see Minutes of the Interactive Session between Northeast Activists and Srimati Swati Maliwal, Chairperson, Delhi Commission for Women held at JNU (see Annexure 3).
12. Constrain of time and resources did not permit us to explore more deeply into these activities. Hence the actions and events documented in this chapter are only illustrative and not exhaustive of the range of activities engaged by the Northeasterners in their attempt to find a solution to their problem.
13. 'SC raps Centre as NE people unsafe in Delhi: Asks if Government is ready to set up Nodal Agency', *The Times of India,* New Delhi, Wednesday, 19 October 2016.
14. 'Racial Violence against NE people: SC grants time to Centre' *The Hindu,* 22 October 2016.
15. Incidentally, in May 2014 Ms. Liyi Noshi was slapped by a group of lawyers at Delhi's Tis Hazari Court when she had gone

there to defend a Northeast woman who was assaulted by a member of their fraternity. At the time of writing this book, the criminal case she filed against the offending lawyers had yet to come up for hearing.

16. The concept 'out-based' has been used in this discussion to refer to Northeast born scholars residing and working outside the region.
17. Vivek Kumar, 2010. 'Different shades of Dalit Mobilization' in T.K. Oommen (ed.) *Social Movements: Issues of Identities*. New Delhi: Oxford University Press, pp. 116–136.
18. For a detailed definition and use of this concept see McDuie-Ra (2012a).
19. According to Foucault, power and knowledge are closely related. In his words, 'there is no power relation without the correlative constitution of a field of knowledge, nor any knowledge that does not presuppose and constitute at the same time power relations' (1978: 27). Though diverging from Foucault on certain points, like him Bourdieu sees a close relation between knowledge and power. While maintaining that power is primarily concentrated in the hands of the dominant class, he shows how the legitimacy of this domination may be challenged and eventually altered by an opposing class by coming up with their own ideology and way(s) of representing the social world (Bourdieu, 1991: 128). See also Foucault (1984).
20. It may also be noted that quite a number of scholars from Northeast are engaged in collaborative research with the best of names in foreign universities and some others are serving as advisors in overseas research on the region.

CHAPTER 7

Conclusion

The present work on the people of Northeast India perceived as the 'other' in India's capital city has yielded valuable information on varied aspects of their life, hitherto obscured by dearth of systematic research. While the argument is based on data primarily drawn from persons hailing from the states of Manipur, Meghalaya and Nagaland living, working and studying in Delhi, the findings throw valuable light on the problems faced by people of Northeast as a whole. Though there is no single cultural and physical criterion that can be used to mark out the people from Northeast as belonging to a distinct group, the construction of Northeasterners as a community is happening in an unprecedented manner in the urban localities and public discourse. There have been certain works that suggest that pan-Northeast solidarity is emerging in cities across India, when social crisis or tragic events that threaten the life of migrants from the region take place in the cities. However, such construction of Northeast identity appears to be sporadic, rather than permanent and structural in nature. Nevertheless, the feeling of oneness by virtue of belonging to the same geographical region is making inroads into the psyche of the Northeasterners in a gradual manner, but in what way this feeling is going to be concretized has yet to be seen.

In real terms, the sense of community amongst the Northeast migrants in the city continues to be in an ambiguous state. At one level, the idea of oneness by virtue of belonging to a single geographical region appears to be strong; but the strands of tribal identity and solidarity have found its presence in the city as well. With the increase in population and presence of people from diverse tribes in the city, the continuation of their tribe-based practices has been made viable. The question that arises is, in the midst of diverse social and cultural environment can the idea of a single Northeast community be sustained? It remains to be seen in what ways the reconfiguration of community will turn out to be. It is plausible to imagine that pan-regional identity may eventually take over as the most viable assertion of community and personal interest in the city where they are a minority in every sense of the term. But till that happens the primordial ties centring on tribe and ethnicity will continue to be the basis on which the Northeasterners structure their relations.

Though the idea of a unified Northeast community remains elusive, Northeasterners have made their presence felt in cities across India not simply as victims of discrimination or the cultural 'other' from the frontier zone, as generally perceived and represented in the discourse by dominant groups, but as politically conscious people aware of their rights as citizens. The process of 'place making', as a mechanism to carve out a niche for themselves in the alien city they choose to make their home, have already been noted by scholars. What we also witnessed is their growing confidence and assertiveness as citizens. Northeasterners have not only become more vocal in expressing their views but also in staking their claim for protection and safeguarding of their interests as promised by the Constitution. The series of memoranda submitted by different civil society organizations, students' associations and women's groups and active negotiations and lobbying with successive governments in the states and the centre point to the Northeasterners' growing political consciousness and assertiveness as citizens. By taking recourse to assertion, Northeasterners are not only staking their rights to the city but also for acceptance of their distinctive social and cultural identity, a fact that finds sharp reflection in a statement made by a young Mizo girl: 'I don't care if they call me Chinky, *Delhi is my city too I have as much right to it as the locals do*. They better accept my face and our distinctive ways, for *I'm as Indian as they are*'.[1]

An important point raised time and again in the discourse on Northeast India is 'race'. People of Northeast are not only seen to belong to a different race (specifically of Mongoloid stock) from the rest of India, race has also been considered to be a major factor in the discrimination against them. While elements of racism cannot be altogether discounted in the problems encountered by Northeast people in India's metropolitan cities, there is a need to refine our methodology in the way in which race or racism is interrogated.

India, in general and urban India in particular, abounds in umpteen diversities and race is just one of such. Therefore, not all acts of physical assaults and attacks on Northeasterners can be viewed through the lens of race. Neither does racism as a practice exists independently of other structures of oppression, such as, caste, class and patriarchy. For instance, the perception of Northeast women as 'morally loose' has little to do with race or the actual behaviour of the observed, as with the ideological structure within which the observer is embedded. Similarly, the opposition shown to the food habits of the Northeasterner has less to do with the quality of the food *per se* or the racial origin of the eaters, as with the association of certain kinds of food with ritual impurity in Brahminic Hinduism.[2] This makes it imperative that we look beyond race into the caste, class and gender dimensions as well, if we are to have a proper understanding of the discriminations experienced by the people of Northeast in the Indian cities.

The role of gender in the violence perpetrated against Northeasterners is well documented in both official records and the popular media, however its nexus with other structures of oppression (caste and class, for instance) has yet to be systematically explored in works on Northeast.

There is also a need to take a closer look at the role of religion in structuring the relations between groups. This is necessary because, on the one hand, religion plays a vital role in providing the social and psychological anchor to believers, especially in times of crisis, exemplified by the supportive role played by the church in the life of migrants in the city. On the other, religion poses major obstacles to intercommunity relations. The growing intolerance of Hinduism towards beef eaters and the conflict it generated between the landlord and Northeast tenants is just one instance. The other is the strong reservation expressed by the Northeast respondents towards interreligious marriage despite their openness to interethnic marriage and intercommunity interactions.

This raises pertinent questions not only about the role of religion as an organizing principle of society, but also about the meaning of 'nationhood' and 'secularism' operative in the country. Evidence reveals that there is a gradual shift in the idea of 'nation' as postulated by the Indian Constitution: as a plural, culturally, ethnically and linguistically diverse entity characterized by equality, fraternity and justice in terms of both opportunity and legal status, with secularism as the mother principle to ensure that no single faith or community is disadvantaged by dint of their poor numerical or political strength.

Today, the idea of nation as a plural entity has been overtaken by the idea of nation as a composite entity where the different elements are fused into one to make a composite whole, in the process numerically small groups and communities located at the margins are completely overwhelmed by the numerically and politically dominant. Accompanying this process is the shrinking secular spaces by the surge of religious fundamentalism across faiths, seriously eroding the principle of secularism enshrined in the Constitution, as a respect for all religions. The problem is further compounded by the increasing use of state power by the ruling class to establish their religious supremacy.

The problems faced by the people of Northeast in Indian cities cannot be disassociated from these processes. In fact, a realistic analysis of the issue indicates that the problem is primarily a consequence of the mindless erosion of the democratic principles, laid down in the Constitution, as the *sine qua non* of a just, liberal and inclusive society. Viewed thus, the challenge before the state for the resolution of the tenacious Northeast problem goes beyond the mere implementation of the administrative measures spelt out by the Bezbaruah Committee and similar committees in their report(s). Rather, it calls for the simultaneous restoration of and strict adherence to the democratic ideals and values enshrined in the Constitution by all organs of the government and institutions of civil society, and a change of mindset in the way in which Northeast and its people are perceived and represented in books, the mass media and policy documents.

In the final analysis, another significant point that emerged from the materials documented in this book, but received little attention in existing works on the subject is the contribution made by the Northeasterners to India's neo-liberal economy and the capital's image as a global city. Though perceived and painted as the 'other', discriminated against at various levels of their life in the city, challenged of their identity as Indians, and maligned as anti-nationals and terrorists, Northeasterners as a category whether back home in the region or as migrants in the cities exhibit little resemblance to the picture of 'anti-nationals' or the exotic and primitive 'other' caricatured in popular imagination. Evidence reveals that the people popularly and collectively called 'Northeasterners' are not only integral members of the Indian

Union, but also constitutes an important work force for the growing Indian economy. However, unlike the mass of economic migrants from India's villages who come to the city in search of livelihood as unskilled or semi-skilled labour in the large construction industry of the metropolis, or as private security guards for the *nouveau riche* and business establishments, or as rickshaw pullers and street vendors among the most disadvantaged, migrants from Northeast India are of a different mould altogether. They not only stand out from migrants of other parts of the country by dint of their race and culture, but also in terms of skills and personal attributes that are most suited for the neo-liberal/post-liberalization economy that India's ruling elite is committed to.

Earlier in the book, mention has been made about the Northeasterners' oriental looks, proficiency in English and dressing mode, which have made them the ideal choice for entrepreneurs keen to project a global image to their business. In an era when business transactions are no longer confined within the boundaries of the nation, the presence of workers with cosmopolitan characteristics who can be hired for a pittance with minimal or no social security liabilities to the entrepreneur is a boon to any business. The large presence of workers from Northeast in malls, BPOs, hotels, hospitals and other service sectors confirms this fact. Yet there is no study that maps the contributions made by the Northeasterners to the Indian economy. On the contrary, Northeasterners have been singled out for attacks for failing to conform to the image of an Indian (whatever that means), and labelled as anti-nationals and morally loose in character.

While such views may have their roots in social and cultural prejudices, they betray a blatant ignorance of India's economic aspirations to be an economic superpower to consolidate its position in the comity of nations as well as to counter the growing influence of China in the South and Southeast Asian region, for which an efficient and dedicated work force is needed. Northeast migrants with their educational qualifications, disciplined work ethics and cosmopolitan appearance and outlook ideally fit this need.

The scope of this book does not permit us to explore more deeply into the issue. However, if we are to have a realistic understanding of the problems the people of Northeast India face and the place they occupy in Indian society, it is imperative that their contributions to the Indian economy and polity are given due attention. If this book succeeds to inspire some scholars to take up the issue in a more systematic and rigorous manner, we will consider the efforts we took to put this work together well rewarded.

Notes

1. It is significant that this statement by the young lady was made at the Delhi Secretariat directly after we emerged from a meeting of Northeast activists with the Deputy Chief Minister of Delhi, Manish Sisodia.
2. We call it 'Brahminic Hinduism' because Hindus in the lower echelons of caste do not strictly adhere to these principles.

Annexures

Annexure 1

Demographic Profile of Northeastern Region as per 2011 Census

States	*Area in Sq Km*	*Total Population (Person)*	*Density per Sq Km*	*Sex Ratio (Females '000 Males)*	*Percentage of Scheduled Tribe (ST) Population*	*Sex Ratio of ST Population (Females '000 Males)*
Arunachal Pradesh	83,743	1,382,611	17	920	68.78	1,032
Assam	78,438	32,169,272	397	954	12.44	985
Manipur	22,327	2,721,756	122	987	40.88	1,002
Meghalaya	22,429	2,964,007	132	986	86.14	1,013
Mizoram	21,081	1,091,014	52	975	94.73	1,007
Nagaland	16,579	1,980,602	119	931	86.48	976
Sikkim	7,096	607,688	86	889	33.80	960
Tripura	10,486	3,671,032	350	961	31.76	983
NER	2,63,179	45,587,982	174	NA	27.70	995
INDIA	–	1,210,193,422	382	940	8.6	990

Source: www.indiaonlinepages.com/pop/states/population of India/html

Annexure 2

To,

Shri Arvind Kejriwal
Honorable Chief Minister
Delhi Secretariat

Respected Sir,

We the entire North East Community (Name of organizations enclosed) congratulate you and the AAM ADMI PARTY for your outstanding success in the recently concluded Assembly Election. We are proud that, we the North East Community had extended full support to your party and this gives us a great hope and high expectation from your leadership. We also believe that the injustice meted to us by this capital city will end once and for all under this people-friendly government. Following are few points we request you to implement, in order to help us attain our rights which had always been denied by all the other political parties which had ruled Delhi.

1. North East support cell at Delhi Government: Appointment of one Senior Welfare Officer under CM Cell headed by a senior officer preferably from Northeast or officer who had served in the North Eastern States. And this officer is mandated to hold meeting once in a month with NE students, NGOs, Social activists, Government servants and state Bhawans to thrash out critical issues.

2. Nomination of one North East Representative in Delhi State Assembly with extra ordinary ordinance or legislation.

3. Initiate for immediate implementation of recommendations made by Bezbaruah Committee for Delhi government and full implementation of recommendations

made by Delhi's Lt. Governor Committee for addressing problems faced by North East people in Delhi.

4. Appointment of one member from North East at Delhi Commission for Women.

5. Appointment of one member each at Delhi Minority Commission and Delhi State Consumer Disputes Redressal Commission from NE community.

6. Removing Hindi as compulsory for recruitment of Delhi Government officials.

7. Immediate passing of Delhi Rent Law.

8. Delhi Govt. to have close tie up with Delhi Police Nodal Officer for North East People in Delhi for redressing crimes, SOS help, prosecution, labour related, education issues, etc. face by northeast people.

9. Land allotment for North East Centre at prime location and funds can be requested from DONER Ministry.

10. Construct more hostels for North East Students at colleges & universities in Delhi. Existing North East Hostel be managed by people/organizations from North East under guidance of panel from Northeast at Delhi.

11. One member from North East at Delhi Chief Minister public grievance cell.

12. Streamlining Delhi Legal Service Authority/ victims compensation to all North East People in time bound manner.

13. Compulsory sensitizing of school teachers and students about information and culture of the North East region.

14. Compulsory sensitization program should be part of compulsory syllabus during teacher training, NCC, NSS, Scout and guide camps. All staffs of Delhi Government should be sensitized at all training schools.

15. Counseling programmes at existing centres by involving north east NGOs for North East crime victims/addicts/destitutes in Delhi.

16. Liberal grant & encouragement for research & studies on problem of northeast people at reputed centre like Jamia Milia NE Studies Centre etc can be roped in

these research / case studies. The studies & research will help Delhi & Central government to frame calibrated policies & schemes for welfare of north east people at Delhi and other cities.

17. Minister ST/ SC may be designated as Nodal Minister for dealing with northeast people's problems and may hold monthly meeting with all northeast NGOs, Women activists, Students leaders and social/cultural organizations.

18. Introduction of syllabus on northeast culture, history, geography etc in all school under Delhi Government like all 1000 of MCD schools.

19. Immediate special voters registration camps for genuine voters at Delhi and Divisional Commissioners may be directed to hold such voters/ ADHAR cards special registration camps by district DCs like one held by New Delhi DC.

20. Labour department to have dedicated Nodal Officer with access to social media to sort out labour-related payments etc. Fast tracking registration of North East Labour Union.

21. Fast tracking trials of cases against NE people by designating Courts for day to day trial for crime like racial crimes, rape, murder, kidnapping cases.

22. To have special recruitment for public prosecutors in northeast states for representing cases in different courts at Delhi.

23. To streamline emergency assistance for northeast crime victims, dead bodies disposal, burial etc, with Nodal Officer for 24×7 assistance.

24. To encourage staff/students exchange/tours/Bharat darshan program from Delhi to Northeast states for better interaction with North East people at grass root.

25. Make it mandatory for providing contract letter to employees of private sectors especially in B.P.Os

26. Inspectors should visit companies to confirm that all required facilities are available and also to check if the company is registered.

27. Labour department should conduct awareness seminars in regards to labour rights and responsibilities of employees.

We look forward to your attention and immediate implementations of the above mentioned point for which we will remain and be proud to have you as our true leader.

Sincerely,

Naga Students' Union Delhi. (President) (G Secy)

Delhi Achik Youth Association. (General Secretary)

Tripura Students' Forum Delhi (President). (G-S)

Arunachal Students' Union Delhi. (Genl Secretary) President.

Delhi Mizo Zirlai Pawl (PRESIDENT) Zohmangaiha (G-S)

All Assamese Students' Association New Delhi.

Manipur Students' Association Delhi

Hmar Students' Association Delhi (President) (Secretary)

Delhi Hmar Welfare Association Chairman. M. Kuy Secrety.

All Bodo Student's Union, Delhi Unit. (President) General Secretary

Dimasa Students' Association Delhi President General Secretary.

Missing Students' Association Delhi Gen Secy

(Vice-President)

North East Support Centre & Helpline, Delhi

Thadou Student Association Delhi — President — Secretary

North East India Forum Against Racism.

North East Trade Union, Delhi — (PRESIDENT) — G.S.

Manipur Young Minds Association, Delhi — Raju Singh (Adviser)

Fight for your Pride 'AAWAHAN' — Sangeeta (CHAIRMAN)

Delhi Police North East Representatives.

LOTHA WELFARE FORUM —

ANAL NAGA UNION DELHI — (WANGHRING RANGANG)

Copy to: J. MINTHANG TIMOTHY — (KUKI STUDENT ORG.)

1. Hon'ble Minister DONER
2. Hon'ble MOS Home Affairs.
3. Hon'ble Sport Minister.
4. Commissioner M.C.D.
5. Lieutenant Governor
6. All Member of Parliament from North East
7. All MPs of Delhi
8. All MLAs of Delhi
9. SC/ST Commission.
10. Social Welfare department Delhi.
11. Press Trust of India
12. A.N.I

Annexure 3

Minutes of Interactive Meeting with Chairperson
Delhi Commission for Women
held at School of Social Sciences I Auditorium, JNU
12 August 2015

1. To discuss the proposed setting of a Special Cell at the Delhi Commission for Women to address the increasing incidence of crime and discrimination against North East women residing in Delhi, an interactive meeting with Ms. Swati Maliwal, Chairperson Delhi Commission for Women (DCW) was jointly organized by NEISW, JNU, the North-East Support Centre and Helpline and North East Forum Against Racism at the School of Social Sciences, JNU on 12 August 2015. Besides the Northeast students and faculty members of JNU, students and faculty of Delhi University and representatives of NE organisations in the city attended the meeting.
2. The meeting began with a brief address by Nodal Officer, North East India Students Welfare, JNU who welcomed the Honourable Chairperson of Delhi Commission for Women and others present at the meeting. She expressed her thanks to the Honourable Chairperson for the keen interest she shows to the Northeast issue and for giving her valuable time for the meeting, despite her heavy schedule. She urged the participants to come forward with their ideas and suggestions to help DCW address the issue in an affective manner.
3. Mr David Boyes Convener, North East Forum Against Racism briefed the audience about the purpose of the meeting and the circumstances that led to it.
4. Dr Alana Golmei General Secretary, North East Support and Helpline shared her concern at the slow pace of the law to address cases of violence perpetrated on the people of Northeast in Delhi and the NCR. Citing 14 cases

(including murder and rape) committed between 2009 and 2014 as examples, she shows how police apathy and bureaucratic hurdles obstructed the delivery of justice at every stage.

5. In her response to the concerns expressed by the Northeast representatives, Ms. Swati Maliwal assured the house that DCW is fully seized of the matter and will try its best to resolve the issue. Stressing that we are not here 'to play politics', she listed a number of measures that she hoped to put into effect to make Delhi a safe place for the Northeast women and men. These include:
   i. Listing all complaints of atrocities on the Northeasterners, FIRs registered and action taken to get the best prosecutors to fight the cases.
   ii. Setting up of 24 - Hour Helpline to provide immediate assistance (in practical, legal and medical terms) to victims of violence.
   iii. Constitution of a special committee comprising concerned individuals from Northeast to monitor the cases filed and to act as a bridge between DCW and the NE community.
6. In the discussion that followed several participants came up with concrete suggestions to strengthen the proposed Special Cell at DCW as well as to alleviate the problems on the ground. The following are some of the suggestions made:
   i. Create Volunteer Groups among Northeasterners to create awareness among new NE arrivals about the problems they are likely to encounter in the city.
   ii. Create awareness in law enforcing agencies/police, officials at various levels of the government machinery and the local population about the distinct culture, history and society of Northeast.
   iii. Integrate lessons on Northeast in the school and college curriculum.

iv. Issue instructions to all firms/industrial units or business employing persons from Northeast to strictly comply with employment norms as per law, or face penal action.

v. Ensure that all workplaces and public institutions set up Gender Sensitisation Committee against sexual harassment as per Supreme Court ruling and the Workplace Act, 2013.

vi. Amend laws to make racist attack legally punishable.

7. The meeting ended with a vote of thanks by Ms. Linda Neumai

Annexure 4

Questionnaire

A Study on the Problems of Northeasterners in Delhi

This questionnaire has been prepared and circulated by North East India Studies Programme, JNU as a part of their research project on studying the problems of Northeasterners in Delhi. The information that you furnish and your personal identity will remain confidential.

(Tick ✓ inside the box wherever applicable)

Name (Optional): Sex:

Occupation:

Religion/Denomination: Place of Origin:

Length of stay in Delhi (w.e.f.):

Language (Mother Tongue):

Number of Languages Known (specify):

Mode of accommodation in Delhi:

(a) Rented ☐ (b) Self Owned ☐
(c) Govt. Quarters ☐

If your accommodation is rented, how did you get the accommodation?

(a) Through Friends ☐ (b) Brokers ☐
(c) By yourself ☐ (d) Others______

1. Did you face any problem in getting a flat/room on rent?

   Yes ☐ No ☐

2. Did you have to pay any security for the room/flat?

   Yes ☐ No ☐

   (a) If Yes, how much is the security? ______________________

3. Are there any conditions laid down by the landlord for giving the house to you? Yes No

   (a) If yes, what are they?

   ____

   ____

4. Have you ever been told by your landlord that you have breached the condition?

   Yes ☐ No ☐

5. In what way do you maintain relationships with people from your community?

   (i) Attending Church/fellowships ☐

   (ii) Participation in Students' Union/Community Organization ☐

   (iii) Living in the locality/area which are populated by people from your community ☐

   (iv) Others specify ______________________

6. Through which contacts do you come to Delhi?

   (i) Friends ☐ (ii) Family ☐

   (iii) Relatives ☐

   (iv) Others specify______________________

7. Have you experienced people passing comments or making judgments about your dressing style?

   (a) Not at all ☐ (b) Occasionally ☐

   (c) Most of the time ☐

8. Have you ever been harassed or made fun of by others about your looks and racial feature?

   (a) Occasionally ☐

   (b) Mostly by Strangers ☐

(c) By Friends ☐

(d) Not at all ☐

9. Do you know anyone else in Delhi besides people from your community?

   Yes ☐ No ☐

   (a) If yes, who are they?

   (i) People in College ☐ (ii) Work/Office ☐

   (iii) Church ☐

   (b) Do you interact with them outside college, work, church, etc.?

   Yes ☐ No ☐

10. Do you feel comfortable in your relation with them (people outside your community)?

    Yes ☐ No ☐

    (a) If yes, in what way do you feel comfortable__________________________________

    ____

    (b) If no, what makes you feel uncomfortable________________________________

    ____

11. Have you ever come across any of your friends or relatives who have faced physical assaults and sexual abuse?

    Yes ☐ No ☐

12. If yes, what are the organizations that are engaged in helping the victims? Specify______________________________

For People at Work

13. How long have you been working here?

____

14. Is the post/position:

    Temporary ☐ Permanent ☐

    Contractual ☐

15. What selection procedure did you go through for your appointment? ____

    ____

16. What are your working hours?

    ____

17. How many holidays in a year do you get (excluding national holidays)? ____

18. Are the holidays the same for all employee in the office/firm/shop etc.?

    Yes ☐ No ☐

19. If no, in what way it is different? Please specify

    ____

20. Have you ever faced difficulties in getting leave for special occasions?

    Yes ☐ No ☐

21. Does your firm provide free refreshment/lunch/dinner for the employees?

    Yes ☐ No ☐

    (a) If no, how do you manage your meals at work?

    (i) Brought from shop/canteen ☐

    (ii) Bring from home ☐

(b) If you brought food from home, do you ever share your foods with your co-worker?

Yes ☐ No ☐

(c) If no, please explain the reason________________________________

(d) Do they share their food with you?

Yes ☐ No ☐

22. Do you face any resentment on their part about the diet/food that you take?

    Yes ☐ No ☐

23. Has anyone commented about the food that you take?

    Yes ☐ No ☐

24. If yes, in what way?

    (a) Jokingly ☐ (b) Depreciatingly ☐

    (c) Others________________________________

On Interaction with the Opposite Sex and Marriage

25. Have you ever had any close relation with a boy/girl outside your community?

    Yes ☐ No ☐

26. If no, please give reason________________________________

27. If yes, please explain the relationship________________________________

28. Have you thought about the possibilities of marrying outside your community?

    Yes ☐ No ☐

29. If no, what are the reasons? Please explain

____

____

____

30. If yes, do you see any problems connected with it?

    Yes ☐ No ☐

    (a) From whom do you anticipate the problem?

    (i) From your family's side ☐

    (ii) From your friend's family side ☐

    (iii) If other, elaborate________________________

31. What is your attitude towards inter-ethnic and inter-religious marriage?

____

____

____

32. What do you think is the most important barrier between the people of North East and rest of India?

____

____

____

33. Do you see similar barriers in the relationship of the different North East communities with each other?

____

____

____

Bibliography

Akoijam, Bimol A., 2012. 'The "Mainstream" and the Northeast: The Curious Case of Contrasting Images', *The Imphal Free Press*, 28 August.

Appadurai, Arjun, and James Holston, 1996. 'Cities and Citizenship', *Public Culture,* Vol. 8, pp. 187–204.

Barse, Sheela, 1996. 'Food Security and Indigenous Peoples' Cultural Rights' in Vilay K. Gupta (ed) *Perspectives on Human Rights,* Delhi, Vikas Publishing House, Pvt. Ltd., pp. 69–80.

Breman, Jan, 1996. *Footloose Labour: Working in India's Informal Economy*. London: Cambridge University Press.

Banerjee, Biswajit, 1983. 'Social Networks in Migration Process: Empirical Evidence of Chain Migration in India', *The Journal of Developing Areas*, Vol. 17, No. 2 (January), pp. 185–196.

Bhaumik, Subir, 2010. *Troubled Periphery: Crisis in India's Northeast*. New Delhi: Sage Publications.

Bourdieu, Pierre, 1991. *Language and Symbolic Power*, trans. Gino Raymond and Matthew Adamson, ed. John B. Thompson, Cambridge: Harvard University Press.

Chowdhary, Prem, 2009. '"First Our Jobs Then Our Girls": The Dominant Caste Perceptions on the Rising Dalits', *Modern Asia Studies*, Vol. 43, pp. 437–479.

Chowdhury, Prem, 2009. *Contentious Marriages, Eloping Couples: Gender, Caste and Patriarchy in Northern India*. Delhi: Oxford University Press.

Datta, Ayona, 2011. '"Mongrel City": Cosmopolitan Neighbourliness in a Delhi Squatter Settlement', *Antipode*, Vol. 44, No. 3, pp. 745–763.

Dube, Leela, 1997. *Women and Kinship: Comparative Perspectives on Gender in South and South East Asia*. New Delhi: Vistaar Publications.

Dupoint, Veronique D.N., 2011. 'The Dream of Delhi as a Global City', *International Journal of Urban and National Research*, Vol. 35 (3 May), pp. 533–554.

Durkheim, Emile, 1915/1976. *The Elementary Forms of Religious Life*. London: George Allen and Unwin Ltd.

Eriksen, Thomas Hylland, 1993. *Ethnicity and Nationalism: Anthropological Perspectives*. London: Pluto Press.

Fong, Eric and Kumiko Shibuya, 2005. 'Multiethnic Cities in North America', *Annual Review of Anthropology*, Vol. 31, pp. 285–304.

Foucault, Michel, 1978. *Discipline and Punish: The Birth of the Prison*, trans. Alan Sheridan. New York: Pantheon (French ed., 1975).

——. 1984. 'The Subject and Power' in Brian Wallis (ed.) *Art after Modernism: Rethinking Representation*. New York: New Museum of Contemporary Art.

Glazer, Nathan, and Daniel P. Moynihan, 1973. *Beyond the Melting Pot*. Massachusetts: MIT Press.

Haokip, Thangkholal, 2012. 'Is there a Pan-Northeast Identity and Solidarity?', *Economic and Political Weekly*, Vol. XLVII (8 September), No. 36, pp. 84–85.

Hazarika, Sanjoy, 2011. *A Measure of Impunity – The Impact of Conflict on Women in Nagaland and Assam*, Centre for North East Studies and Policy Research, Delhi: Jamia Millia Islamia.

Horowitz, Donald L., 1985. *Ethnic Groups in Conflict*. Berkeley, California: University of California Press.

Judge, Paramjit, 2012. 'Love as Rebellion and Shame: Honour Killings in the Punjabi Literary Imagination' (Special Article), *Economic and Political Weekly*, Vol. XLVII (3 November), No. 44, pp. 44–50.

Kalpagam, U., 2008. 'Marriage Norms, Choice and Aspirations of Rural Women', *Economic and Political Weekly*, 24 May, pp. 53–63.

Kanungo. Pralay, 2008. 'Hindutva's Fury against Christians in Orissa', *Economic and Political Weekly*, 13 September, pp. 16–19.

——. 2012. 'Hindutva Combats Christianity in Orissa', *Purushartha*, 30, CEIAS/EHESS, Paris.

Kleniewski, Nancy, 2005 (ed.). *Cities and Society*. USA: Blackwell Publication.

Kumar, Vivek, 2010. 'Different Shades of Dalit Mobilization' in T.K. Oommen (ed) *Social Movements: Issues of Identities*, New Delhi: Oxford University Press, pp. 116–136.

Lin, Jan, 2005. 'Community, Ethnicity, and Urban Sociology', in Nancy Kleniewski (ed.) *Cities and Society*, USA: Blackwell Publication, pp. 100–109.

Madan, T.N., 1965. *Family and Kinship: A Study of the Pandits of Rural Kashmir*, Bombay, Asia Publishing House, Second revised edition. Delhi: Oxford University Press, 1989.

McDuie-Ra, Duncan, 2012a. *North East Migrants in Delhi: Race, Refuge and Retail.* Amsterdam: Amsterdam University Press.

——. 2012b. 'The North East Map of Delhi', *Economic and Political Weekly*, Vol. XLVII (28 July), No. 30, pp. 69–77.

Nath, V., 1988. 'Studies in Migration', *Economic and Political Weekly*, Vol. 23 (21 May), No. 21, pp. 1061–1066.

Nongbri, Tiplut, 2003. 'Ethnicity and Gender: Identity Politics among the Khasi' in *Development, Ethnicity and Gender: Select Essays on Tribes in India*, Delhi and Jaipur: Rawat Publications, pp. 229–267.

——. 2014. *Development, Masculinity and Christianity: Essays and Verses from India's Northeast.* Shimla: Indian Institute of Advanced Studies.

Ota, Satoshi, 2011. 'Ethnic Identity and Consumption of Popular Culture among Young Nega People, India', *International Journal of Asia Pacific Studies*, Vol. 7, No. 3 (2011), pp. 53–74.

Pachuau, Joy, 2010. 'On Being Mizo': A Re-analysis of Issues of Identity from India's Northeast, Ph.D. Thesis submitted to University of Oxford, United Kingdom.

Ramesh, Babu B., 2012. *Migration from Northeast to Urban Centres: A Study of Delhi Region*, Noida, NLI Research Study Series, V.V. Giri National Labour Institute.

Raj, Sushani, 2012. 'Loving and Living in 21st Century India', *Economic and Political Weekly*, Vol. XLVII (23 June), No. 25, ISSN (Online), pp. 2349–8846.

Robinson, Rowena, 1998. *Conversion, Continuity and Change: Lived Christianity in Southern Goa*. New Delhi: Sage Publications.

——. 2003. *Christians of India*. New Delhi: Sage Publications.

Said, Edward, 1978. *Orientalism*. New York: Pantheon Books.

Sarukkai, Sundar, 1997. 'The "Other" in Anthropology and Philosophy', *Economic and Political Weekly,* 14 (July), pp. 1406–1409.

Sassen, Saskia, 2005. 'Overview of the Global Cities', in *Cities and Societies,* Nancy Kleniewski (ed.). USA: Blackwell Publication, pp. 83–90.

Singh, K.P. and Shakeel Ahmad, 2012. 'Taking Stock of Higher Education in the Northeast', *Economic and Political Weekly,* Vol. XLVII (22 September), No. 38, pp. 24–26.

Srinivas, M.N., 1952. *Religion and Society among the Coorgs of South India*. Oxford: Clarendon Press.

Thounajam, Swar, 2012. 'A Preface to Racial Discourse in India: Northeast and Mainland', *Economic and Political Weekly,* Vol. XLVII (11 August), No. 32, pp. 10–13.

Varadarajan, Siddharth (ed.), 2002. *Gujarat: The Making of a Tragedy*, India: Penguin Books.

Viswanathan, Susan, 1993. *The Christians of Kerala: History, Beliefs and Ritual among the Yakoba*. Chennai: Oxford University Press.

Vithayathil, Trina, and Gayatri Singh, 2012. 'Spaces of Discrimination: Residential Segregation in Indian Cities', *Economic and Political Weekly,* Vol. XLVII (15 September), No. 37, pp. 60–66.

Weiner, Myron, 1993. 'Rejected Peoples and Unwanted Migrants in South Asia', *Economic and Political Weekly*, Vol. 28 (21 August), No. 34, pp. 1737–1746.

Wirth, Louis, 1927. 'The Ghetto', *American Journal of Sociology,* Vol. 33 (July), No. 1, pp. 57–71.

——. 1938. 'Urbanism as a Way of Life', *American Journal of Sociology*, Vol. 44 (July), No. 1, pp. 1–24.

Reports

Bezbaruah, M.P., 2015. *Report of the Committee to Look into the Concerns of the People of the North East Living in Other Parts of the Country*, Government of India.

CNESPR, 2014. Discrimination and Challenges before Women from North East India: Case Studies from Four Metros New Delhi, Mumbai, Kolkata and Bengaluru, A Study conducted by Centre for North East Studies and Policy Research, Jamia Millia Islamia, New Delhi.

NESCH, 2011. *North East Migration and Challenges in National Capital Cities,* A Research Report by North East Support Centre and Helpline, Delhi.

Nongbri, Tiplut, 2011. *Country Technical Note on Indigenous People in India with Special Focus on the Northeast Region,* NEISP, JNU, Project Report commissioned by Asia Indigenous People's Pact (AIPP), Thailand on behalf of International Fund for Agricultural Development (IFAD), Rome.

Newspapers

The Telegraph, 10 July 2007.

Times of India, New Delhi, 5 March 2014.

Times of India, New Delhi, 19 October 2016.

The Hindu, 3 February 2015.

The Hindu, 22 October 2016.

First Post, 27 May 2015.

Index